02/08/2013

To My Josh

I don't know w...
you showed up, but ...
so glad you did. My
life is greatly ~~in~~ enhanced

STDs: Sexually Transmitted Demons, 2013 Edition
Copyright © 2008, 2013 by Laneen "Dr. Intimacy" Haniah
Library of Congress Control Number: 2013901092
ISBN: 978-0-9794210-4-4

Scripture quotations:

Holy Bible. New Living Translation copyright © 1996, 2004 by Tyndale Charitable Trust. Used by permission of Tyndale House Publishers.

Holy Bible, New Kings James Version. Copyright © 1982 by Thomas Nelson, Inc. Used by permission. All rights reserved."

Acknowledgements:

To Yahweh, My Father in Heaven: Thank you for this life-changing revelation and choosing me as the ordained vessel to share it with the Body of Christ.

I thank the father of my children, Emmanuel Haniah, for always being a great supporter and father to our children.

I thank the late Bishop Moylan Jackson for your love and support when I was still an undelivered Mary Magdalene.

As always, I am thankful for the love and support of my family: My Mom Elder Gail Thomas-Wilson, and my two sisters Karmina Dai and Jamila Wilson.

Thank you Prophetess Brenda Todd and Brother Tom Todd for helping me to define the specifications of my Kingdom assignment.

Creative Solutions R BEST

TM

Dedications

I dedicate this book to every young person who reads it: the young in age, the young in heart and the young in spiritual development. This is the stuff that no one taught me. I won't let the same thing happen to you!

And also to:

My seven children: My eldest son Ja'Keim; My daughter Nebiyah; My son Benjamin; My son Judah; My son Zechariah; My daughter Mi'Kara and My daughter Anayvah. I pray that you will reap a harvest of purity from this seed that I am sowing into other young lives.

Who is Yeshua? Who is Yahweh?

For the most part, I only use Jesus' originally given Hebrew name, which is Yeshua[1] (yeh-o-shoo-ah). I also use The Name of the Father God Almighty, which according to Exodus 6:3[2], in the first and original King James Version of the Bible, is Yahweh/Yah (YHWH). He is also known by Elohim, El Shaddai, Adonai, El Elyon and many other wonderful names. Yah says that we ought to exalt His Name, and this is why I use His Name Yahweh many times throughout the book. Also, I have purposefully spelled satan's name with a lowercase 's' throughout the book. I will even break literary rules to defame him. He gets no honor in my life! This is just FYI (smile).*

***Important Note**: If you feel so led in your heart, please skip ahead at any time during the reading, to page 94 in order to find out how you can become a born again believer in Yeshua Ha-Mashiach (Jesus Christ).*

---

[1] Jesus' originally given Hebraic name has a variety of different spellings. This is my preferred spelling of those that I found listed in my research. The same is true for the name of the True God Yahweh.
[2] Also Ps 83:18, Isa 12:2 & 26:4

Contents

What's Up People!

Get ready, get ready, get ready young people because you are about to learn stuff that you probably never knew before! Yeah, I know that you probably think you know a lot already. You probably definitely think you know a lot about sex (even though your Momma doesn't know – *shhhh* – don't worry I won't tell.)

The problem is – **the <u>SOURCE</u> of your information**. Everything you've learned about sex has probably been taught to you by either of the following:

A) Your parents — watered down gibberish, designed to downplay the whole "sex thing".

B) Your Health Ed teacher — politically correct gibberish, designed to meet "tolerance" guidelines.

C) Your friends — ignorant and hyped up gibberish, designed to make you think that they know more than you do.

It's time to get the real scoop! I'm here to give it to you ***raw and real***: THE TRUTH ABOUT SEX! No holds barred and nothing held back. I'm about to lay it on you. So turn off all of your electronic gadgets: MP3 player, Play Station, Wii, computer, cell phone – all of that stuff. Kick back and get ready to be blown away by what you read.

I got messed up at a young age, being raped and molested at age two. I lived a wild life. I had sex with a lot of people. I experienced a lot of pain. *And,* I learned a lot of truth that I want you to be able to use for your own success when it comes to sex. Nobody in church wanted to tell me the truth, but you will never have that excuse after reading this. You probably haven't ever heard a preacher get this real and this open and break it down like this – trust me on that!

Your Girl Who Keeps It Real,
Dr. Intimacy

NOTE TO PARENTS, TEACHERS, AND PASTORS – ALL LEADERS

*Every year I get thousands of visits to my website from young people who are in some kind of "trouble" with their sexuality. Many of these young people reach out to me needing answers and help, not knowing where to find it. I am sorry to disappoint you if you think otherwise, but **they are not likely to talk to you about it**!*

When my pastor first read this book, she was shocked by the rawness of it. She is "old school" Baptist and it was a bit much for her. However, I am so thankful that she trusted the Anointing on my life and my understanding of my assignment. She has since enjoyed learning of the deliverance and healing of many young people. Even many older people that missed important steps in their spiritual and emotional development have gotten a breakthrough from reading this book.

The cover is raunchy and provocative – and believe me – the content is not any softer. Nevertheless, please understand that I have been doing this for over a decade now, and I have come to understand that people that are deeply bound by sexual sin feel too guilty to pick up a Bible. Many of them will never step foot in a church and they are certainly too ashamed to seek counseling. Sinners, backsliders and babes in Christ feel like those of you who "have arrived" cannot relate to their struggles. Furthermore, they cannot understand scriptures, their attention span is short, and they long to be entertained.

This book is "rough on the religious". I admit it. Just please try to remember who this book is written for. Those who need it are drawn to it because of the cover; they are captivated by it because of the content; and they are transformed by it because of the message. If you can just look past the method and focus on the message, I assure you that you are going to be grateful for this book and the way that it is written. It will reach those that you never could and make your job as a leader, who has to deal with sex issues, that much easier.

In the Power of His Love,
Prophetess Laneen "Dr. Intimacy" Haniah

~ Chapter 1 ~

So Who the Heck Are You?

kay, so question number one is who the heck am I, right? Let me just tell you that I am someone you should listen to! That may sound cocky, but hey if I don't believe that about myself, I will never convince anyone else of it. So I say to you again, "*I AM SOMEONE THAT YOU SHOULD LISTEN TO!*" Let me tell you a little story to break the ice and prove to you that I am someone that you should definitely listen to – at least when it comes to sex and things like that.

It was the spring of 1990. I was fifteen years old and it was the night that I was about to lose my virginity. In case you don't know – that means that I was about to have sexual intercourse for the very first time. I know most chicks want it to be a "special experience" when they lose their virginity, but I didn't care about that junk. I just wanted to get laid.

I hated being a virgin. To me, virginity was like a curse; it was like having the cooties; it was like being left out of the party; it was being the only one in the cafeteria wearing a school uniform when everyone else was decked out in the latest video fashions; it was being out of style and out of the loop! I hated it! I know that sounds crazy to some and familiar to others.

I had wanted to lose my virginity for a while, but had been too scared to go through with it. Besides, I was definitely NOT one of the popular chicks. I didn't even have a boyfriend, so how was I supposed to accomplish sex? I mean, there were some dudes that wanted to get with me. But you know – they were like the nerdy, unpopular and...*ugly*...type – *ewww!*

I wasn't an ugly girl. The only reason that I did not have any guy of significance checking me out was my size. I was extremely small for my age. You see, I had gotten sick at the age of eight-years-old. I ended up with a disease called Lupus. The disease was unbelievably destructive. It wrecked my childhood and my body. Actually, I was not expected to live, but all thanks to The LORD, I did.

However, I did not get over on the consequences. I lived, but I did not get away *scot-free*. The result of the disease was that I looked like I was a little girl when I should have looked like a teenager. When all of the other girls were blossoming and budding into shapely, sexy young ladies; upping their bra sizes and finally fitting into their Momma's jeans; I was still shopping in the little girl's section at Wal-Mart.

At fifteen years old, I honestly could have passed for eight or nine, that's how small I was. Not only was I short and skinny, but I also had no chest, no hips and had big, fat baby cheeks. It was terrible. Instead of getting asked on dates, I was getting pinched on my cheeks by dudes with comments like, *"Aww, Laneen you so cute. I'm gonna call you my little sista."* When guys that I had a crush on did stuff like that to me, I can remember thinking, *"I don't wanna be your little sister, I wanna be your freak!"*

Don't be shocked that I am telling you this. I told you that I'm going to keep it 100% in this book!

So anyway, it was spring time in 1990. School was going to be ending soon. You know we get the "crazies" when school is about to be over with for the year. I don't know about you, but there was always something about the summer that seemed to stir up my hormones. Once the heat hit, I would get "horny as hell" *(or horny with hell is more like it!)*

Besides that, my sixteenth birthday was right around the corner. I was determined to hit sweet sixteen as a "woman", a broken-in, sexually experienced woman. This was my goal. I had to lose my virginity before I turned sixteen and before school was out for the year.

Getting laid before the school year ended was critically important to me. Once school was out, there would be no way for me to contact all of the cute guys that I wanted to get with, *unless* I got their phone numbers before the last bell rang. However, I knew that there was no way that those guys were going to stay in contact with me over the summer without a good reason.

I wanted to give them that good reason to stay in contact with me. I wanted to ditch my virginity and then spread the news around the school. Then all of the guys would know that I was 'sexable'. That would get their attention, for real. I mean, it was just a fact that all of the popular girls at school were the ones that "gave up the goods". I wanted to be one of those girls.

Unbelievably, I was actually trying to get *a reputation*. Man was I a fool! *Getting* a reputation was easy; but *getting rid* of it once I realized I didn't like having one was **impossible**. I know that now, but

I always say, ***"Hind sight is 20/20 vision that sees nothing."*** Hind sight is useless and it certainly didn't help me. On that mild spring night, sometime in May of 1990, I lay down on my bed, opened up my legs and let all hell enter into me.

That first experience was terrible. It started off with me getting "advice" from one of my knuckle head friends. She was **THE School Nasty Girl** – I mean she literally carried the title. She also happened to be my best friend, and I wanted to be just like her. *Can anybody say, "Bad company corrupts good character" (1Cor 15:33)?* That's a scripture straight out of the Bible, and it's *fo' real y'all!*

If there was anyone to teach me how to get a reputation, "Lisa" *(not her real name)* was the girl to do it. When I told her what my goal was, she went to work to help me come up with a plan to make it happen. Since I didn't have a man at the time, she looked in her rolodex of former sex partners to select some candidates for me.

Lisa, who was 16 years old, had been sexually active with at least 40 guys at that time, so we had a lot of people to choose from. I can remember the process of elimination we went through. It was sad, but it is actually kind of funny reminiscing on it *(so laugh with me please)...*

Lisa: *"...So Laneen, let's pick someone to bust yo' cherry. OK, not this guy he's way too big for you."*

Me: *"How about him Lisa?"*

Lisa: *"No, his breath stanks girl!"*

Me: *"Well, what about this one?"*

Lisa: *"Umm, maybe, he cums kind of quick though. I mean, do you want it to last long so you can cum too?"*

Me: *"What the heck does that mean?"*

Lisa: *"You know, have an orgasm — climax girrrl!"*

Me: *"I don't know how to do that."*

Lisa: *"Well don't worry about that. It can take a while to learn. Let's just get through step one for now."*

Me: *"What do you think though Lis'? I mean a minute-man might work for me because that way if it's hurting, at least I'll know it'll be over with quick..."*

We went through this process until we finally chose the 'lucky winner'. Not being in pain was my **primary** concern. I still had Lupus and even though I was not as sick as I had once been, I still had a lot of pain in my body. I was very fragile. The dude we chose, according to Lisa's review of his performance, met the following criteria:

He had a medium-sized penis. He wasn't too rough but had nice skills. He was fun to hang around and wouldn't put pressure on me. He was fairly clean with no BO (body odor). He was older so there would be no time restrictions as far as him having to be home by a certain time. And he was in our circle of friends at school, so he would definitely spread the news.

That's a pretty pathetic way to decide who to give the precious gift of your virginity to, don't you think? But, that's how it went down.

The sex itself was terrible. I didn't know what I was doing. I had been watching porn, taking tips from Lisa and reading a lot of romance novels. I really wanted to *freak him*. I wanted him to give a good report to the fellas in the lunchroom about how I rocked his world. But it was whack – *I* was whack.

First of all, I did not have the feel of a virgin and that really shocked and disappointed him. Lisa had explained to "Theo" *(not his real name)* my situation, so he was expecting to break-in a virgin. I was *technically* a virgin. I had never had intercourse or any kind of sexual contact with a guy – well not other than being molested and raped way earlier in my life.

However, I was so afraid of having my cherry popped by a penis that I had actually been *practicing sex* long before that night. I actually thought it would be a good idea to bust my own cherry. (There is a piece of skin called the hymen that covers the vagina until it is penetrated the first time. Breaking that piece of skin is referred to in slang as "busting" or "popping the cherry" because the female bleeds when that piece of skin is broken.)

For months leading up to that night with Theo, I would insert different objects into myself. I did this using a slightly bigger object each time until something that was about the size of a – larger than average – penis was able to easily go into me. It wasn't until I accomplished this that I informed Lisa that *I was ready*. I know that sounds gross, and it was. I don't want to get any more graphic about that than I have already. So, let's just say that when it was all said and done, there were some vegetables missing out of the icebox!

OK, there you go with your mouth hangin' open again. Didn't I tell you that I was going to keep it raw and real in this book?!! Popping my own cherry is what I thought I needed to do because the first time a girl has sex; it can be and usually is a painful experience for most females. I did not want to experience that pain.

Anyway though, once Theo realized that I didn't have the *vajayjay* of a virgin, it became just about the mechanics of the sexual act. Pain wasn't even an issue. I had stretched myself out enough for him to slide up in me with ease *(smh - shaking my head)*. As we were sexing, I wanted to try out all of these different things on him, so I could *freak him*. Plus, I was remembering what Lisa said about having an orgasm, and I was trying desperately to do that too. I can remember this puzzled expression on his face throughout the entire encounter, maybe even more like a look of pity...

Go ahead y'all, please keep laughing with me cuz' my face is red as a tomato right now, LOL.

So, now that I have your attention, now that we've broken the ice...

Let me just tell you that I have to laugh through this, or I feel like I will just die of humiliation! Who really wants people to know stuff like this about themselves? No one does! I'm no different. However, I share these types of stories all over the country, on the internet and in the books I write. People think that it's easy for me to put myself out there like this because I flow so well with it, but believe me – it's not easy.

So why do I do it then? I do it because somebody has to tell the truth! I am a licensed Christian Minister, Evangelist, Preacher of the Gospel of Jesus Christ and a Yahweh-ordained Prophetess of The Kingdom. I am also a mother of seven beautiful, well-behaved children, a respected businesswoman and an accomplished author – *and more good stuff, yadda, yadda, yadda....* However, none of those accomplishments erases the fact that I am a woman with a nasty and dirty past. This is the truth my young people.

But you know what? I am not the only one; I am only one of many. I am sure plenty of you reading this right now can relate to my story in some way or another. If you can, or even if you can't, believe me when I tell you that there are tons of adult men and women hiding behind families, successful business careers and clergy collars; trying desperately to escape the truth about their past (and sometimes their present).

Somebody has to be willing to be a voice of truth, and I signed up for the job. Sometimes I like my job, sometimes I dread it – but I am committed to doing it all the same. I am committed because I care about you. I learned some stuff in my dirty days. I learned something that can help you right now, right where you are.

Are you still a virgin? I can help you! Have you lost your virginity? I can help you! Are you sexually inexperienced? I can help you! Are you really sexually "out there"? I can help you! Have you been molested or raped? I can help you too!

It doesn't matter where you're at in this thing. The information that I am about to share with you can change your life forever. I mean it can change it for the better and save you from a lot of unnecessary problems down the road. So let's get ready to do this! *Are you wit' me?*

~ Chapter 2 ~

Sex Changed My Life!

My life changed – my life changed dramatically after that night. I can literally pinpoint the changes that occurred in my life to that day and hour that I first had sexual intercourse. After that horrific, yet comical, first-time sexual experience that I had – **MY LIFE CHANGED DRAMATICALLY**. What most people don't realize is that <u>**SEX CHANGES YOUR LIFE**</u>. It doesn't change it just a little bit either. Sex changes your life very dramatically and very specifically.

The reputation that I wanted to gain – a reputation as a sexable freak that would easily give up the goods – came almost instantaneously. I wish everything I desire in life would come so quickly. And, it's funny how wishy-washy we can be as young people sometimes. The Bible calls that being "double-mined" because I didn't even really want what I was asking for.

Even though I wanted Lisa to teach me how to be a nasty girl, I was often disgusted by some of the things that she told me she did. When she would tell me about her sexcapades, I would be thinking to myself, *"Ilk, I'm not ever gonna be that nasty!"* That's what I said, but I didn't understand that having sex would ***enslave*** me the way that it did. It enslaves everyone who falls prey to it – and sex is a hard taskmaster once it owns you.

I cannot remember exactly when my next sexual encounter took place, but I know that it was within a couple of weeks. A boy from school called me, due to my *hard-earned* reputation. He had heard about my encounter with Theo. I came to find out later that one of the main reasons that no one in the school wanted to have sex with me was because of my small size, and because they all knew that I was sick. Everyone was too afraid that they would hurt me. Nevertheless, once dudes found out that Theo had broken me in; and that I did not break into pieces during the sex; they lined up to get their turn.

By the way, Theo took a bad rap at school because everyone wanted to know from me if the sex with him hurt. When I told them that *"it didn't hurt at all"*, everyone assumed it was because he was a 'pee-wee'. I felt bad for Theo; but I thought it was better for everyone to think that he was packing light, than for them to find out that I had been packing vegetables! [3]

I left Theo out to dry. And unbelievably, the fact that he was trying to defend his manhood by telling everyone that I was not really a virgin when he sexed me; yet me insisting that I was; made everyone very curious. It actually helped my cause. That made guys want to *do* me even more. They all wanted to judge for themselves, whether or not I was "fresh meat" or "old microwaved chuck steak".

So anyway, this guy named "Dave" *(not his real name)* called me from school. He was really sexually deranged. He used to talk about sex every day at the lunch table. He would tell stories of how he

---

[3] Funny update: I became a top leader in a company that I worked with. I facilitated the local training meetings where guest were encouraged to come and hear about the company. I almost fainted when Theo, whom I had not seen in 20 years since that night, walked into the room. I am usually really suave and cool, but I came completely unglued when I saw him! LOL

would stick pencils into the rectum of his gerbils and watch them have orgasms. He said they would usually die after the orgasm because of the intensity. *Can somebody say "sicko"?*

When Dave called me, I was surprised. He had never called me before. He told me that he had gotten my number from Lisa. I couldn't stand Dave. He was pesky and annoying. It seemed like he was a little "sweet" too, if you know what I mean. Besides that, he was ugly as sin. It's not right, but the typical teenager is vain and shallow. I was no different – looks were important to me, and Dave was torture on the eyes.

The night that he called me, the first evidence of how sex had changed me became real. It was kind of late in the evening when he called. It was almost time for me to go to bed. He was begging and begging me to meet him outside. I was like, *"What for?"* He just kept saying that he wanted to talk to me. I didn't want to go meet him outside. I didn't like talking to Dave. But you know what... **I could not say 'no'.**

The inability to say 'no' was the first thing that I noticed about how sex changed me. I had always been a real feisty, independent person. I was not easily pressured into anything, and I was a leader – not a follower. I was defiant and confrontational. I loved to say 'no' to people, just for the sake of being confrontational and independent. The very idea of me not being able to say – **no** – was insane.

The second thing that I noticed is how having sex broke the bond between me and my Mom. Let me explain to you what I mean by that. Yahweh's plan for sex is that it happens with a man and a woman that are committed to each other in marriage. The Bible says that when a person gets married, they are supposed to leave their mother and father and cleave (cling and bond) to their husband or wife. *(Eph 5:31)*

Remember what I was telling you about "popping the cherry"? Well, that piece of skin that covers a female's vagina is placed there by God as a seal. Her husband is supposed to break that seal on their wedding night. Once that seal is broken, she and her husband enter into a covenant (or contract). Once they enter into that covenant with each other, the covenant that they once had with their parents is broken.

Ok, stay with me because this is going to get a little deep for a minute...

You see when you were born, you entered into a covenant with your parents. First, you developed inside of your Momma's belly, in what is called an *'amniotic sac'*. That sac was filled with a water-like substance called *'amniotic fluid'*. The fluid contained life-sustaining nutrients, particles of your blood cells, skin, bones and everything else concerning your development.

The amniotic sac acted as a seal. Before you entered the earth through birth, you were **sealed** in a covenant with Yahweh God. Everything you needed to survive was contained inside of that amniotic sac – your connection to life (the umbilical cord); nourishment (the amniotic fluid); and shelter (the fluid and sac itself).

This is a picture of how you are fully sustained **in** The LORD. As you remain sealed **in Him**, you have everything you need to survive. You come from inside of Him. That is why the Bible says, *"I knew you before I formed you in your mother's womb... (Jer 1:5)"* And it also says, "...*just as He chose us* ***in Him*** *before the foundation of the world... (Eph 1:4)"* As long as you were sealed inside of that sac in your Momma's belly, you never made contact with her blood, and she never made contact with yours. Once blood is mingled, covenants are created. New covenants often times break old ones.

I believe that The Father's heart aches when He sends us into the earth; like sending your child off to war. He knows He must let us go and do what He created us for, but the separation hurts Him. I believe that is why He keeps us sealed within that sac during our fetal development. That sac – and the entire developmental process that occurs in the womb – prevents the Mother's blood from ever mixing with the baby's blood, and therefore preserves our covenant with Him.

The Creator wanted to hold onto you until the very last moment. He knew that once that seal was broken that He would have to release your spirit, and let you enter into blood covenant (contract) with your parents. They would then replace Him as the sustainers of your life from that point forward. They would become your covering, providers and source of nourishment. He used your time in the womb to form you for survival and prepare you for success, downloading all of the wisdom and empowerment needed for you to fulfill your purpose.

When it was time for your Momma to deliver you, your protective seal broke. For the very first time since you were conceived, your Mom made contact with your blood. The fluid that was inside of your sac, which contained particles of your blood cells, gushed out of her womb. Some of it leaked out of her body, some of it was absorbed into her system. As you passed through her birth canal, you made contact with her blood for the first time as well. As a matter of fact, you were born covered in your mother's blood from head to toe.

In the Bible, the strongest and most important covenants (or contracts), were established in blood. A covenant, once established in blood, can only be broken by new blood or by death. So at birth, the intermingling of you and your mother's blood temporarily broke the covenant that you had with God as Your Father in eternity. The intermingling of your blood sealed you two into a new covenant.

In addition to that, since the Bible teaches us that a man and woman *"become one"* when they have sex; you were automatically entered into covenant with your father, through the covenant with your mother. What many people do not understand is that saying "I do", at a wedding ceremony is not what causes two people to become one. Having sex is what causes two people to become one!

Every time you have sex with someone, you enter into a blood-sealed covenant with that person – you enter into a marriage. *(I will explain this more later in chapter 7).* Therefore, regardless of whether your mother and father were married when they conceived you, they were still **ONE**. So there you have it, you were born, and suddenly a covenant was created between you and the two people that would be your biological parents.

Ok, so let me bring this all back home by getting back to my story about Dave...

The night that Theo and I had sex, I entered into a blood-sealed covenant with him. Remember, every new blood covenant breaks or amends any conflicting covenant that was created before it. I therefore, broke the covenant that was established between my parents and me at birth, when I had sex with Theo. Being in covenant with him broke the bond and connection between me and my Mom. I am telling you all of that to say, where as I would never have lied to my Mom before I had sex, it was nothing for me to lie to her after I did it. The bond between us was broken. I was not under her protective covering anymore.

Whenever you are in a contract with someone, that contract protects you. The purpose of a contract is to make sure that all of the people that enter an agreement are protected and treated fairly. Any good contract is going to establish benefits and responsibilities for all of the people that are bound by it, on both sides.

Since everyone involved in a contract has something to gain, and something to lose if the contract fails; the people that are sealed into the contract are going to look out for each other. They are going to **cover** each other – you know *have each other's backs*. However, when someone breaks the contract, then the people in the contract do not have to cover each other anymore.

When I broke contract with my Mom, by having sex with Theo, I placed myself under his covering. The only problem is, Theo didn't give a hoot about me. He offered me no type of protective covering at all. So what I really did was put myself out on the edge of a cliff! I put myself out there in the world on my own.

Of course, I did not understand all of what I am telling you now back then. Nonetheless, even though I could not break it down like I can now – I *knew* that something was different. I could feel it. I felt like I was not a child anymore. I felt like I had to make my own decisions regardless of what my Mom had to say. I couldn't explain it, but I just knew that I was not bonded to my Mom anymore.

So when Dave called, I found myself unable to tell him 'no'. Realizing that I could not tell him 'no', as he pestered me about meeting him outside, I had a new problem. *How in the world was I going to get my Mom to let me out of the house at that time in the evening?* The devil was right on my shoulder. He had a handy lie ready and available when I needed it. Before I even realized what I was saying, I opened up my mouth and said, *"Mom, I am going to go outside to take out the garbage."* I honestly did not even think about. It just came out. It was a reflex of my newly earned independence.

My Mom definitely thought that what I said was odd. I hated taking out the garbage. She usually had to beg me to do it – and in the dark no less! There were often rats and stray cats around the garbage cans. It was scary. She was suspicious. However, I was very persistent, telling her that it had something really stinky in it. She gave in, and I was out the door. *I wish, I wish, I wish my Mom would have known I was lying. I wish she would have said, 'no'...*

I met Dave outside. I handed him the garbage, *"Here, take this to the trash bin."* I said to him. He didn't even find it strange that I handed him a bag of garbage. He knew what time it was because I had told him on the phone that I was going to have to come up with an excuse to get out of the house. As we walked to the garbage can, Dave was asking me questions about my sexual experience with Theo. I was really uncomfortable with the conversation.

Then he started asking all kinds of questions about sex in general. He wanted to know what kind of positions I liked. He wanted to know what kind of guys I liked. He wanted to know what size penises I liked. He inquired about the size, shape and feel of my vagina. He wanted to know if I had ever "eaten out" a girl. I couldn't believe he went there with the girl thing. I was like, *"Ilk, you nasty freak! No, I haven't eaten out no girl!"*

Thinking back on it, I realize now that Dave was really probing me – trying to figure out whether or not I was lying about being a virgin when I had sex with Theo. As we talked, he told me to keep walking with him. We were getting further and further away from my house. I had told my Mom I was going to take out the garbage; I didn't want to walk that far away from my house.

However, the curse had come on me – I just could not tell him 'no'. So I walked with him, complaining all the way. It was chilly outside. I was not dressed for a long walk. I had come out dressed for a short trip to the garbage bins. But I followed him... *and followed him...* until at last we stopped.

I looked around. We were in the vacant parking lot of a store. I had been there once before to buy my Mom a Mother's Day gift; many years earlier in my days of innocence. It was all starting to make sense to me now. Dave didn't live anywhere near me. He had walked to my house. It had to have been at least a 30-minute walk from where he lived. It suddenly dawned on me that he had not come out just *to talk*.

No horny, teenage boy is going to take a 30-minute walk just to talk! At the end of the day, no matter how many questions he asked me, only one thing was going to settle his mind. The only way he was going to know for sure if I had told the truth about being a virgin, was to have sex with me. I said to him, *"Why did you bring me here?"*

He answered me very plainly, *"So I could f#%k you."* His straightforwardness both shocked and frightened me. Lisa had already had sex with Dave. She told me that he had *"a really big one"*. I DID NOT want to have sex with Dave. She said he was rough too. I could not have been more afraid. Yet at that moment, I was about to see evidence of the third way sex had changed my life: **doing things that I always said I would never do**.

Lisa had told me plenty of stories about having sex outside. I thought that it was so nasty. I said I would never do it. It did not take too much more convincing on Dave's part though, to get me to fulfill his request. He told me that he was not going to let me go home until I let him "stick it in". He begged; he pleaded; he almost cried; he even threatened. He made false promises too. He promised that he would not *have sex* with me. He said he would just *"stick it in and feel inside"*. I told him that I had to get home. He promised that he would be quick.

Finally, I laid down on the cold concrete; out in the open; under a brightly lit street lamp; in full view of a main road and all who might pass by; and let him do what he wanted to. *Oh gosh was I sorry!* He had tricked me. Dave must have had sex a million times before that night because what he did had to take practice. It seemed like in about 10 seconds flat, he had somehow used my own clothes to restrain me. Like I said – **PRACTICE**!

He did a lot more than just "stick it in". He was flat out sexing me, and he had no intentions of *just getting a feel*. He wanted a full-blown orgasm. I asked him to get off of me, but he wouldn't. Lisa was right too – his penis was huge. It was hurting the heck out of me. I was moaning and screaming, begging him to get off of me.

At that point, I felt like I was being raped. I don't know if legally that would be considered rape or not because I did initially give him permission, but it certainly felt like rape to me. I even started to scratch him hard and deep to try to make him get off, but it seemed like my pleas for mercy were only turning him on more. In addition to the pain from the intercourse, I was also in pain from the weight of his heavy body. The cold concrete that was underneath me was scraping against my skin and bruising my fragile bones.

I was still sick and still suffered from a lot of pain in my body. What he was doing to me was brutal, but there was nothing that I could do about it. I was completely trapped. I thought he was going to kill me. I wondered how long it was going to last. Every second seemed like an eternity. Every forceful jab into my vaginal canal sent shudders through my body, and I just could not take any more.

I was disgusted by the sight of his hideous face and the rotten smell of his breath. His animal-like grunting made me feel as if I was being raped by a gorilla. Then... *eureka!* I had a plan. I remembered Lisa telling me that every dude's favorite position was doggy-style. I remembered her demonstrating the position for me so I would know what it looked like.

At that thought I screamed out to Dave, "*Wait! Let's change positions.*" It was the first time that he had paid attention to anything I said, since he had gotten on top of me. But my conniving intelligence won out over his lust. When I told him that I wanted to do it doggy-style, he was more than willing to get off me. I was so relieved when he finally got up. I pulled my clothes up in record time. He was like, "*What are you doing?*"

I said, "*I'm going home.*"

Then he said, "*But you told me you wanted to do it doggy-style.*"

"*Well, I lied to you just like you lied to me. I told you that I needed to get home. I'm going to get in trouble. Besides, you didn't stop when I told you that it hurt, so forget it.*"

Dave could have easily overpowered me and finished his rape. I don't know why he didn't. It must have been The LORD looking out for me. I walked back home in much pain. Dave followed me all the way. He was still trying to convince me to "let him finish". He even tried to tell me that I should sneak him into my house, but I wasn't going for it. The one thing that would empower me to be able to say 'no' was my fear of pain.

As I got closer to the house, I was feeling bolder. I told him that if he didn't leave, I was going to tell my Mom that he was bothering me. That finally made him leave. Isn't that funny – *the very one that I had lied to, in order to get into that bad situation; I then wanted to call on to help rescue me?*

I never would have carried out my threat to tell my Mom though. Like I said, the bond with her was broken. I had removed myself from her covering. I did not feel like she would protect me or even **could** protect me anymore – even though I know she would have tried, if I had only reached out. But the truth of the matter is, I needed protection from *myself* more than Dave or anyone else at that point. I was about to become my own worst enemy.

That was the first of many nights that I would find myself not being able to say **'no'**; lying to my Mom; and doing things that I said I would never do. It would not be the last time that I got raped either. It wouldn't be the last time I had sex outside. It was just a very faint foreshadow of things to come. That was just the *initial* proof of how much sex had changed my life – how much sex had changed **me**.

Sex changed me on the inside. The devil was just getting started...

Why Can't I Say 'No'?

*A*fter the summer was over and school started again, I continued my sexcapades. I was quickly catching up with Lisa, threatening to take her crown as **"THE School Nasty Girl"**. She was jealous of all of the lustful attention that was being poured out on me. That had always been her benefit as the queen of reputations. But all of a sudden, every dude in the school wanted his chance to bang "Freaky Little Laneen".

I think I did eventually take Lisa's crown. I sexed just about every guy she had sexed, and more. But trust me when I tell you, it was not a victory that I celebrated. I would have gladly given her the title back – I mean **GLADLY**! Everything in my life continued to go *down, down, down...*

Everybody noticed the ugly changes in me. I wasn't even the same person anymore. Something evil was on the inside of me. It had taken over my life and I could not control it. Every day, I found myself doing something else that I said I would never do.

I was under the curse – I could not say 'no'. I didn't know why, but it seemed like a fact. The Bible says in Romans 6:16, *"Don't you realize that you become the slave of whatever you choose to obey? You can be a slave to sin, which leads to death, or you can choose to obey God, which leads to righteous living."* That first choice that I made to obey

the lust in my body made me a slave to sexual sin f<
come. I was under the curse of sin and it certainly wa
death.

This train wreck – this bondage to sin – went on in my life for the next seven years, until I finally gave my life to Yeshua, the Lord Jesus Christ. Some people seem so laid back when they get Born Again. I don't know what their story is, but I know for me it was a life or death decision. I was utterly desperate, and if things didn't change, I was going to die. By the time I was finally ready to do what every human being on this planet was created to do – let The LORD control my life – it almost seemed like it was *"too little, too late"*.

By that time in my life, at 22 years of age, I had become a drug addict, dealer and gang member, and had been in jail several times. I was placed in several mental institutions. I had a gun put up to my head on four different occasions. I was raped repeatedly. I got jumped and stabbed. I had practiced witchcraft trying to protect myself. I ended up being a high school drop-out and teenage parent. I had then become a stripper and a prostitute trying to support my son. I eventually had sex with many people and contracted sexually transmitted diseases on numerous occasions. Because of all of this drama, three different times I made very serious suicide attempts!!!

Yes! All of these things happened to me after I started having sex. I didn't know what was going on. I didn't know how to break the cycle of negativity. On that day in particular, when I gave my life to Yeshua, on September 29, 1997, I was living with a married man who was an alcoholic. We had been together for going on two years. He hated my son and was physically and sexually abusing me.

In a desperate effort to "fix" things, I decided to end the lives of both

...e and my three-year-old son. I was planning on committing murder-suicide. Little did I know that it was my day for change; for a breakthrough; and a new beginning. Unable to go through with my plan, I did what seemed to me at the time ridiculous – **I cried out to The LORD.**

Sobbing uncontrollably I said, *"God, if you will just be real to me I will serve You. I'm tired of the testimony of others about how good You are. I want You to be real to **me**. I don't need religion. I am lonely and hurting and broken, and all I want is a friend who loves me. Will You be that to me? Will You be real to me?"* I was totally amazed and *sooo* drunk with happiness and surprise because God responded to me immediately with His very presence. I literally felt Him wrap His arms around me. I stopped crying right away and my life was never the same.

After that, I was totally in love with My Savior. From that very moment that Yahweh God wrapped His arms around me – my life began to change. One day you saw me, and I looked like I was about to work a 5th Avenue street corner. The next day, after my conversion to Christianity, I came out looking like I was about to go on a mission's trip with Mother Theresa!

I knew how to look the part, but it didn't take long for me to see that I didn't know how to live the part. Something had changed in my heart – it really had. Every day I lived just to spend time with my new Friend; it was so awesome. For a few months, I was doing great. I had kicked out my alcoholic boyfriend and I had no man in my life at that time.

In the seven years since I had started having sex, I had never gone more than four weeks without sex. It wouldn't even have been that long had it not been for my time in jail and mental institutions. So imagine how proud I was of myself to pass the two-month marker. It was the first time – since the "first time" – that I had been able to maintain that long.

I really thought that I was going to be okay. What I didn't realize though is that the only reason I was not having sex was because I had isolated myself from people. I was enjoying my new life with Yahweh so much that I had completely shut everyone else out. However, the day I started mingling with 'church folk', all of that would change. So much for my two month "no sex streak" – that is as long as I was going to make it.

I wanted to be a *good girl*; I really did. I wanted to believe that I had changed. I faced an ugly reality when I started going to the church though – people in the church were just as much slaves to sex as I was! The first ministry I joined, I ended up having sex with one of the Associate Ministers. The next church I went to, it was the Assistant Pastor. The same old life, just in a different package – I still couldn't say 'no'.

It was a painful experience, especially the situation with the Assistant Pastor. However, if we allow Him to, Yahweh will use everything in our lives to get glory for Himself. I say this because through the sexcapade that I had with the Assistant Pastor, I finally began to understand why my life had become so unpredictably bad – I finally started to learn what I needed to know to be able to write this book for you today. I finally learned why I couldn't say **'no'**. So let me tell you the story...

...It was September, 1998. We were having an Indian Summer day in New York. I loved those types of warm days, so I decided to go to church. It had been about one year since my conversion. Unfortunately, I was in a terribly backslidden state at the time. For the first six months after I got Born Again, I was fine. But I didn't last too long after I had sex with the Associate Minister of that first ministry I linked up with.

I had a crush on the minister, and quite honestly had deceived myself into thinking that he wanted to marry me. He fed the deception by telling me that he was "trying to choose" between me and another young lady. He was full of crap though. He had already made his choice. He was just stringing me along trying to figure how he could get away with sexing me.

At the very least, I thought men in the church would respect me, but I was wrong. He and I had known each other for seven months at the time that our relationship took on a different face. The other young lady that he was considering marrying was supposedly a virgin. She was 23 years younger than him too. I guess I – as a washed up, used up, sexed out single mother – never stood a chance against the young and fair maiden!

He used me for sex so he could help maintain his precious virgin's purity! The night that we had sex, after he finished he said to me, *"Now when Diane comes, I'll be all right."* She was on her way to visit him in just a week or so because she lived in another state. Can you believe the pig said that to me? I was so angry!!! *(You can read the full version of this story in my other book,* **"The Spirits of Sexual Perversion Reference Book".***)*

That experience led me to believe that I was still the same old slut that I had always been. If not even a minister would have respect for me then what chance did I stand? If the leaders in the church did not respect me; if they saw no value in me; if they did not love me – did God? I mean, weren't they supposed to be a reflection of Him? Therefore, I eventually left the ministry and turned my back on the LORD.

About six months later on that Indian Summer day in September of 1998, I went to a different church. I had no desire to repent, or pray, or get my heart right. I honestly went to the church because number one, I had nothing better to do; and number two, I wanted to show off. I had actually joined this church a few months before I backslid. They all seemed to want me to be a member. They were religious but nice. I felt loved there by most of them. I hadn't been back though in about six months because of the thing that had happened at the other church.

The devil told me that they were all talking about me, even though they had nothing to do with what had happened at the other ministry. I thought that I needed to show them that I was doing fine without them! I went dressed to kill, in a very sexy dress. I looked like a doll baby – I kid you not. I had my little man, my cutie-pie son, hooked up too.

After all of my lustful profiling, I caught the attention of the Assistant Pastor. I can't say that I blame him. I was so deep in sexual sin at that time that I was drowning in it. Lust was dripping off of me everywhere I went. He followed me out of the church and asked me if I wanted a ride home.

I didn't want a ride home. It was such a beautiful day outside and I looked so cute. I just wanted to enjoy the day and enjoy my vanity.

Besides that, I didn't want no *"freakin' sermon"* on how I was living, and how much I needed to get back into the church. I know that's raw, but I'm just keeping it real. That is how strongly I felt about it.

He kept persisting though, so I finally got in his car. *The sermon started... I was annoyed... He asked for my number saying he would give it to his wife so she could "minister" to me...* I was thinking to myself, *"Yeah, take my number and let me get the hell out of this car please!"* I convinced him to let me out at the train station instead of driving me all the way home.

Little to my surprise, it was not his wife that called me. It was him that called. That day, by the time I got home, he had called me six times. I was used to these so-called "men of God" though. I called them "niggaz of God". After my encounter with the Associate Minister, there had been many others that tried. There was even an occasion when I had lesbian sex with a female Minister, and there were more of them that had tried too. So... no, I was not surprised when he called me.

I need to shorten up this story because it's a long one. Let me fast forward. I had about a six month, non-sexual relationship with him. I thought he was a dork at first. He dressed old fashioned, and had slicked back hair like Elvis, *like OMG!* But during the time frame that he was pursuing me, I began to want to return my heart to The LORD.

The dorky Pastor suddenly became the only person in my life that I could talk to about God because I never went back to the church after that day of showing off. He always wanted to sex me; that was apparent from the beginning. But I was not going for it. At that time, I was into women as a preference. I had zero interest in having a relationship with any man because I had been hurt so many times. The only way I was going to have sex with a man was if he paid for it!

But Good Lord, "Elder Tony" *(not his real name of course)* was a persistent little pest. Funny though, after a while, when I wanted to get right with Yahweh, I was glad that he was in my life and that we had never had sex. Over time, I really got close to Yah again. I really wanted to make it living the Christian life. I cut everybody off again and I stopped having sex and using drugs.

Elder Tony was the only person in my life. I could feel myself wanting to fall with him and I tried everything I could to get him to stop checking me. I knew that I could only go so long without sex. It had been months, and I knew how much he wanted me. I did not want to blow my relationship with God again; I did not want Tony to blow his position in the church or his marriage to his beautiful wife.

I begged this man to leave me alone, and I mean begged with tears. For two months before we had sex, I asked him persistently to please end communication with me. Then I begged The LORD to make Elder Tony go away. I begged Him to keep me from falling. I knew that we would fall if he stayed around me. I knew that I would not be able to say 'no' the day he finally asked me for my sex.

However, he never heeded my warnings because he wanted to fall. A little over six months after the day he had me in his car, we had sex. I had fallen again. But something different happened that time – Yah opened up my eyes! Every time in my life that I started getting close to Him, sex would always pull me away from The Father. I would always turn and run, but not on that occasion. I was about to turn and run from The LORD like I always did, but He didn't let me.

Tony and I sexed several more times and then God Himself ended our relationship. That day that we last had sex, Yahweh said to me something like, **"I'm going to raise you up to teach my people about sexual perversion. You will deliver my people."** I understood that day why He had let me fall with Elder Tony.

You see every other time in my life, other than the times that I was raped, I always wanted to have sex. Even though I hated doing it, I had a "love-hate" relationship with sex. I hated doing it, but I wanted to do it anyway. I always believed, *"This time it will be different."* That experience with Tony was the first time that I really, really, really – in every part of my heart and mind – did not want to have sex, but ended up doing it anyway.

It was this fact that finally opened my eyes to understand that the urge to have sex was about more than just a longing throb in my womanhood that yearned to be satisfied. Yes, my body craved for sex with Tony – but for the first time my heart said no, and my soul said no. I knew it was wrong and dangerous and detrimental – and I DID NOT WANT TO DO IT.

And out of that broken place in my heart, Yahweh spoke to me. He said to me,

"Daughter, don't you understand that there are demons that control you? There are spirits of sexual perversion that drive you. That is why you can't say 'no'. But I'm going to teach you how to fight. I'm going to teach you how to stand. I'm going to teach you how to run. I'm going to teach you how to be victoriously free from every demon of sexual perversion."

~ Chapter 4 ~

The 'X' in SeXXX

olling back to my teenage years... That summer that I turned sixteen, I got the birthday present I had wished for – everybody knew that I was a ho – I got "a reputation". Before the summer ended, I think I had been sexed by about ten different guys. *Some present I gave to myself – don't you think?*

Most of the sex, I was pressured in to. I never enjoyed any of it. I was either in pain, or just bored; I was zoned out from start to finish every time. I never had one of those wonderful orgasms Lisa had told me about. I hated it – **I HATED HAVING SEX**. The porn movies and romance novels had lied to me! I had been tricked; duped.

Losing my virginity was not what I thought it would be, and I wished I could have it back. I wished I could never have sex again. But, I had placed myself under ***the curse*** – the "I can't say no" curse – the curse of sin. Every boy that asked, if it could be done without us getting caught, got what he wanted. And believe me, as the word got out about me; more and more guys were asking.

It was a very quick, downward spiral into the depths of sexual bondage...

- ✓ I thought having sex would put me in control of my life.
- ✓ I thought that it would make me grown up – a woman.
- ✓ I thought it would cause me to be stronger.
- ✓ I thought it would make me more popular.

Having sex didn't do any of that for me. As a matter of fact, it did just the opposite in all areas.

- ✓ My life got so out of control, so fast. It was like I got hit by an express train. I didn't know whether I was coming or going.
- ✓ Even though I had broken the bond with my Mother, I didn't feel like a woman. I felt as much like a little girl, as I had when I was five.
- ✓ I didn't feel stronger. I felt just as weak and vulnerable as I had when I was in a hospital bed for months, not knowing if I would live or die.
- ✓ And certainly, I was not more popular.

The few friends that I'd had before becoming sexed-out, I lost. They all lost respect for me. The only thing that I ever really had going for me was my innocence. The thing I hated so much – my small, child-like stature – is the thing that actually made me unique and likable. Once I lost the innocence that was expected to go with my size, no one had any interest in me anymore.

...Be careful, because the thing you hate most about yourself, may be the very thing that Yah has given you to make you stand out and uniquely shine!...

All of my male friends wanted to screw me. My female friends wanted to stay away from me. Even Lisa became jealous of me. She thought that I was trying to put the moves on her boyfriend. He was not even my type – *okay*! But, I lost her too. My relationship with my mother was already pretty rocky before I had sex, but what little of it was left to salvage, was quickly demolished afterward. She too lost respect for me and because I had broken the contract with her, I got out of my place as a daughter.

I became a sad, lonely and lost little girl. I had made a mistake – a terrible, terrible mistake. I was slammed by the reality of what having seXXX was really all about.

Does any of this sound familiar to you? Why does life get this way after we have sex? What really happens? Just think about it – I bet you know someone right now that used to have a pretty decent life until they started having sex. Now that person's life has gotten crazy and ugly. If you don't know someone like this yet, you will soon.

So what happens when we have sex that makes life get this way? Why does SEX CHANGE YOUR LIFE?

Before I answer that question, let me explain something to you. I know you must still be wondering why the title of this book is **"STDs: Sexually Transmitted Demons"**. I mean after all, we are already into the fourth chapter of this, off-the-chain-book, and I have not even mentioned demons.

We are going to get to that – I promise – and it is going to blow your mind! But first, I want to make sure I lay all of the ground work. I really want to help you understand what seXXX is really all about. I'm not telling you these crazy stories about my past just to entertain you and turn you on. **"Hey! This is not a porn book, okay!"**

So, what I need to let you know before we move on is what makes sex – seXXX. What activities really meet the qualifications of being "sex"? I really have to go here. And, I'm going to have to be just as raw about this as I have been so far – *so don't you go start with your mouth hanging open again – LOL.*

I run a lot of youth meetings; I get hundreds of e-mails from people; and you would not believe the kind of stuff that comes up on my blog (http://drintimacy.wordpress.com)! It never ceases to amaze me that people are so deceived about what makes sex – seXXX! I mean *"real sex"* when I say "seXXX" because a lot of people think that certain activities are not real sex.

Let me explain what seXXX really is, and what I mean when I say "sexual activity". You will see that term "sexual activity" in this book, and you need to know what it means. I need to be very clear on this because a lot of people think that as long as the penis does not penetrate the vagina then seXXX has not taken place. This is a lie and a deception!

SeXXX and "SeXXXual Activity" include:

- Vaginal intercourse – penis penetrating the vagina.
- Anal intercourse – penis penetrating the rectum.
- Oral sex – when the mouth makes contact with the male or female genital area. *(The genital area includes the penis, testicles, butt and surrounding area of a male; or the vagina, labia [vaginal lips], clitoris, butt and surrounding area on a female.)*

- Manual sex – when the hand makes contact with male or female genital area.
- Using any type of object to deliberately cause sexual stimulation and/or arousal (i.e. vibrator, sex toys, clothes, lotions, etc...).
- Humping and/or grinding – standing, laying or sitting (with or without clothes on) with your genital area in contact with another person's body and then making movements with the intent (or knowing) to sexually stimulate and/or arouse.
- Sexually stimulating rubbing of the body (especially when touching the breast, chest, butt or thighs).
- Tongue or body kissing done with the intent, or to the point of, sexual stimulation and arousal.
- Mutual masturbation – when two people touch their own genital area, together at the same time, in order to sexually stimulate themselves and each other (including phone sex.)

It may surprise some of you that all of the above acts are included in "sexual activity"! However, you have to understand that the 'X' in SeXXX begins in your heart. I may not be kicking a lot of scriptures or going all "John the Baptist" on you (*YET – wink, wink).* However, make no mistake about it; this is a Christian book; based on Christian principles; having in mind those that want to live the Christian life!

In Yahweh's eyes, seXXX begins in your heart, where your desire to do the wrong thing or the right thing is born. I told you we are going to keep it raw and real in this book right? So stop playing yourself by thinking that you can involve yourself in all kinds of seXXXual activity, like what is mentioned above, and still lift up HOLY hands on Sunday morning in the church!

And while I'm busy busting yo' bubble of deception: Let me tell you also that you do not have to have an orgasm – or "cum" as you probably call it – for seXXX or seXXXual activity to have taken place. It is still seXXX even if you don't have an orgasm. The lust in your heart makes it seXXX before you ever make a move...

I'm not about being a prude – trust me. I was married for 11 years after my encounter with Elder Tony. I learned to enjoy sex; I actually came to **love** it! *(Can't you see my big, cheesy grin?)* In my other book, ***"The Spirits of Sexual Perversion Reference Book: 2013 Edition"***, I dedicate an entire section to having great, mind-blowing sex in marriage. However, I do represent the Gospel of Yeshua Ha-Mashiach and The Kingdom of Yahweh God. Therefore, I have to explain things to you in the way that God sees them, not in the way that society sees them.

People in our society may tell you that it is okay to do the things that I have labeled as seXXXual activity. We are basically taught in society that any sexual activity that is done "safely" is okay. Well I'm sorry to disappoint you, but in Yah's eyes it is not okay – it is sin. The LORD looks at the intent and motive of a person's heart. When you engage in seXXXual activity, the motive of your heart is to achieve seXXXual pleasure in a different way than how God intends for it to be done.

~ Chapter 5 ~

Attacked & Invaded During Sex

Now finally, I can get down to the nitty, gritty! You ought to trust me enough by now to know – I am not some religious chick; throwing a lot of Bible jibber at you; just to big up my own chest! It took a long time for me to really get cleaned up and delivered after that experience with Tony. But, I was so determined to become the deliverer that Yahweh God promised me I would be.

The first book that I wrote was called **"The Spirits of Sexual Perversion Handbook"**[4]. I love that book; it has blessed so many people. It will always be one of my favorites. However, I didn't write it with young people in mind. When I think back on those dark, confusing days of my life as a teenager, young adult and new Believer, my heart really aches. That is why I wanted to write a book that would really minister to you as a young person or new Believer. So now it's time to get into "the meat" of this book's message!

---

[4] You need to read the other book after you read this. In that book, I give the total breakdown of everything that I first learned about the demons that influence our sexual behavior. That book is *God's Handbook on Sex Education – The Encyclopedia of Christian Sexuality!* You can check it out on my website or on Amazon.com. It has recently been updated and republished under the title, *"The Spirits of Sexual Perversion Reference Book: 2013 Edition"*.

QUESTION: WHY DOES LIFE GET SO MESSY AFTER YOU HAVE SEX? WHY DOES SEX CHANGE YOUR LIFE SO MUCH?

ANSWER: YOU GET STDs.

I'm not talking about the kind of STDs that they teach you about at Planned Parent Hood. Not the kind that people **claim** a condom can protect you from. No – I'm talking about an STD that no condom can protect you from. The person who's carrying it will show no physical signs that you can recognize: You won't smell it or feel it, and even though you will see it; you won't realize what it is.

I am not talking about a sexually transmitted disease. What I'm talking about is worse than a sexually transmitted disease. There is no medical cure for the STD that I'm talking about – no pill to pop, or shot you can get. What's even worse is that with this STD, you usually get multiple forms of it at one time.

WHAT ARE THESE STDs THAT I'M TALKING ABOUT? THEY ARE SEXUALLY TRANSMITTED DEMONs!

No! I am not kidding you. I am as serious as cancer. Sexually Transmitted Demons are just as real as sexually transmitted diseases. Do you know that that *everyday 8,000 teens are infected with a sexual disease? But you can't tell when you look at them right? *1 out of every 4 teens is infected with some type of sexually transmitted disease: Herpes, gonorrhea, syphilis, chlamydia, HIV and others that are less common. But most of the time you don't know it when you look at them. *(*www.megmeekermd.com © 2008)*

Just like you can't actually see the diseased cells that are inside of a person's body, you can't see the demons that they carry with them. But just like those disease cells are there, so are the demons. If you could tell someone had a sexual disease just by looking at them, wouldn't you avoid having sex with that person? Of you course you would! But the reason that so many people catch sexual diseases is that they cannot tell the person they are having sex with is infected just by looking at them.

Remember, I told you in the first chapter of this book that I am someone that you need to listen to! So please believe me when I tell you that just like you cannot see those sexually transmitted diseases, neither can you see those Sexually Transmitted Demons! But they are there; they are real; and they are what causes sex to change your life so drastically.

Okay, let me slow it down just a bit. Let me explain to you exactly what a demon is. I know you have a lot of stuff in your brain already, so I'm going to keep it as simple as possible.

Demons, to put it very simply, are evil spirits. A spirit is a living being that does not have a physical body, kind of like a ghost. When a spirit wants to do something in the physical world, it needs to *borrow* someone's body. When I say "physical", I mean the world that you can see, touch, taste, hear and smell. In other words – the world you interact with through your five senses.

Demons try to get into people so they can use a person's body to do things in the world. If they cannot get *into* a person's body to use the person in that way, they will try to do it another way. They will hang *around* the person. By hanging around the person, they wait for an opportunity to *influence* the person to do bad things. Demons have a voice; they can speak to your mind to influence your thoughts and behavior.

Demons and the influence that they have on people are the cause of every bad thing that happens in life and in this world. Of course, I am not saying this to release anyone from being responsible for their own actions! You have the authority to keep demons from using your body, and you do not have to give in to their negative influences. You can choose to do the right thing.

It may be hard to believe that demons are real because you cannot see them. But hey, you believe in a lot of things that you can't see. When someone farts in class, you can't see that, right? But you believe in that fart because of the negative effect that it has in the room! *(We needed a little laugh break, hehehehe.)* You don't actually see the gas that is passed, but you experience the effects of it.

Demons are the same way. Even though you cannot see demons, you do experience the effects of demons. Demons have a negative and evil impact on the world. That is why when a person becomes infected with STDs – Sexually Transmitted Demons – the effects are always negative!

No one ever changes for the better when they start sexing. You always see that person start going downhill: drug use, slipping grades, more problems at home, increase in depression, etcetera... Some, or all and more, of these kinds of things happen to people when they become sexually active. Just think about your own life, if you are already sexually active, or maybe the life of one of your friends. *Hmmm...*

In case you haven't gotten it yet – **I am saying that demons can be transferred from person to person during sex or sexual activity!**

Okay – so If you're still with me, and you believe what I am saying; you must be wondering exactly how it happens. If we can understand how something works, then we are better prepared to protect ourselves from becoming a victim. That is why educators spend so much time explaining what sexual diseases are and how they are spread.

So, I want to give you the full scoop on these spiritual STDs and how they work. Knowledge is power, fo' real! Or, more specifically:

*"**Learned** and **APPLIED** Knowledge is Power"*.

You know what AIDS is right? AIDS is the worse disease that you can get from having sex. AIDS is one of the leading killers in our world today, especially for people in your age group.

I know that 'STDs' usually stands for "Sexually Transmitted Diseases"; but in a spiritual sense, they stand for **"Sexually Transmitted Demons"**. I know that **AIDS** usually stands for "Auto Immune Deficiency Syndrome". But when I think about AIDS in a spiritual sense, it stands for – **"Attacked & Invaded During Sex"**! **AIDS** is what happens when you have sex or even engage in sexual activity – you get attacked and invaded by the demons that are carried by your sex partners.

Remember throughout the rest of this book:

STDs = Sexually Transmitted Demons

AIDS = Attacked & Invaded During Sex

This may all be sounding a little crazy to you. *Where am I getting this stuff from?* Well, I can refer you to my own life experiences to begin proving my point. But first, let's recap:

- ✓ Demons are bad.
- ✓ They need to use someone's body to do their evil works.
- ✓ If we do allow them to use us, we are going to do bad things.
- ✓ Any influence that demons have on us will be a negative one.

So with that in mind, let me tell you more of what happened in my own life after I started having sex...

I can remember how much I hated cigarette smoke as a child. People were constantly smoking around me, and I was forced to smell and breathe the smoke. I hated it! My stepfather used to like to kiss me on the lips. I liked his kisses, but I hated the stench of cigarette smoke that always lingered on his mouth. I swore that I would never, ever smoke.

My passionate determination to never smoke cigarettes increased all the more when a "prevent cigarette smoking in children" campaign started. I saw a video on how cigarette smoking destroys your body and can lead to death. I was absolutely horrified to learn this. I wondered how and why people would do this to themselves.

However... when I was 15 I started sexing a boy who smoked cigarettes. Within just a few months of having sex with him, I too began to smoke. I don't even know how or why I started smoking. I did not even like smoking. But it was an **STD**. I received a demon of addiction when I had sex with a cigarette smoker.

I can remember being a straight A student pretty much throughout school. I was one of the "smart kids" at school. I was one of the ones who was on the stage for almost every award that was called out. I was always a candidate for academic competitions to represent my school. School was important to me. I enjoyed school.

However... when I was in the eleventh grade, I started sexing a boy who had dropped out of school. Guess what? Just a few months later in the twelfth grade, I dropped out of school too. You cannot call it "peer pressures" either because I was no longer dating the dude when I actually dropped out. What happened? I was infected with an STD. I was attacked and invaded by his demon of failure.

Another example would be my involvement in crime. We had our problems growing up, but I did not live in a home where drugs were used or where the main influencers in my life were criminals and welfare recipients. My mother worked hard, and she was a beautiful, classy woman of integrity. She raised us to respect ourselves, each other and the law.

However... when I was 17, I started sexing a guy who sold drugs and stole. Guess what? Not long afterward, I began to sell drugs and steal too! I caught an STD. I was infected with his spirit of crime – the *thug spirit* as I call it.

The list could go on and on:

- After sexing an alcoholic, I too became an alcoholic.
- After sexing a homosexual, I too became homosexual.
- After sexing a racist, I too became a racist. Etc., etc., etc...

In all of the above cases, I had received an STD. I had become infested with some type of demon or demonic influence. I had been Attacked & Invaded During Sex!

Have you ever had a thought or just done something strange that really caught you off guard: something that made you ask yourself, *"Where in the world did that come from?"* Did you notice yourself change after you got into a sexual relationship? Do people tell you that *"you act just like so-and-so"?* Have you done things that you swore you would never do?

These are all signs and symptoms of STDs operating in your life.

The Breakdown

In 1993, just two years after I had begun my life of sexual addiction, my life was an absolute mess. I was only 17 years old and I had already had three sexual diseases. I was no longer going to school at that time. I had dropped out in the twelfth grade, just a few months before I would have graduated. I was on my second apartment. I had gotten kicked out of the first one for not paying rent. That was probably a good thing. It had become nothing but a haven of drug dealers and sex addicts.

After getting kicked out of that apartment, I went to stay with relatives and "friends". Everywhere I went, I left a trail of destruction. No one wanted me in their house for more than a couple of months. The forces of evil were operating so strongly through me that my very presence would change the atmosphere in people's homes.

When I was finally able to get another apartment of my own, I moved into one of the worst neighborhoods in town. I lived upstairs. Directly downstairs from me lived two crack addicts, with their children. I had stopped selling drugs for a while, but with the pickings being so ripe, I was bound to get back into the game. The devil sure knows how to set us up for failure. I really could not have been in a worse environment. Anywhere there are drug addicts, there is prostitution; and where there is prostitution, there is every kind of sexual perversion known to humanity.

With me already not having the power to say no to sex, this was not a good place to be. The type of people that I had been having sex with up until that point, were basically teenage boys. They had not been too "out there" yet. But I had just moved into an arena where I would begin to have sex with grown men, who operated in a greater level of perversion.

The men were older and had been exposed to more sexual partners. Exposure to more sexual partners meant that they carried more STDs. Most of them were Jamaican drug dealers and were known to have sex with prostitutes. Although my life was already bad, it was about to get way worse than I could have ever imagined.

I began to date one of the drug dealers. He was a drug "King Pin" in town. I became his "Drug Queen", so I really got entrenched in the drug and gang culture. Everybody cheated, on everybody and with everybody. That is just the way that it was. At the end of a profitable day, there was plenty of drugs and alcohol to go around and that always led to – seXXX.

If your boyfriend or girlfriend was around when you got horny, then fine. But if not, *"What the heck! Just bang the next available person or prostitute and keep it on the 'down lo'."* Nothing was ever really kept on the *down lo* though. They talk about "loyalty among thieves", but that's bull! There is no loyalty in satan's kingdom – everyone is out for themselves.

Rumor had it that my boyfriend had sexed a prostitute. I figured it was true, but *what did I care?* He was married anyway, so I was already used to the idea of him having sex with someone else. As long as he came back to me, I was cool with it. When he was away, I had my flings too.

It became obvious that the rumor was true because he contracted Chlamydia from the prostitute. He then in turn infected me with it when we had sex. When I had my next fling, I passed the Chlamydia on to my fling buddy. I wonder who he had sex with after me that he then infected with Chlamydia*???*

STDs work a lot like sexual diseases.

When my boyfriend infected me with Chlamydia, it did not cure him of it. We both ended up with the disease. Chlamydia is a viral infection. It infects your body when even just one cell of that virus passes into your system from your infected sex partner. That cell then multiplies, and you end up with a whole bunch of the disease cells in your body.

Once you are good and contagious, when you have sex with someone else, you will infect them with Chlamydia. When you infect that person; you don't give them all of the disease cells that are in your body. You pass a handful of the infectious cells along to them, while the ones that are left behind in your own body continue to work and multiply.

Then the same process that caused you to be infected happens in the person that you have passed the diseased cells along to. The cells that you passed along to him or her multiply. When that newly infected person has sex with someone else, they keep most of the multiplied virus cells in their own body, while spreading a handful along to their new and unfortunate sex partner.

Demons often come in clusters just like the virus cells that cause a person to have a sexual disease. So if you have sex with someone and they pass along to you a spirit of addiction *(drugs, alcohol, gambling...)* they don't suddenly get cured of addiction. They pass to you one or two of the many spirit**s** *(plural)* of addiction that are at work in their life, and they keep the rest.

The fact is that there are many demons that go by the same name. Names of demons are not "Proper Names" in the way that you might think. They are categorical names. For example, a demon of pornography is not properly named 'Pornography Jones' (like a Bob Jones). The term "pornography demon" is simply used to categorize that particular type of demon.

It's just like if I say, *"I like citrus fruit."* The term "citrus fruit" is not the actual name of any particular fruit. It is a term that is being used to categorize a certain type of fruit; acidic fruits, that grow on trees and are rich in vitamin C. I am explaining this to help you understand how someone can transmit a demon of some sort to you and yet still keep the same demon themselves. They pass to you that "type" of demon, while they keep some of that same "type" for themselves.

There are 10 major categories or types of sexual demons:

1. **Fornication** – all illicit sex or sexual activity.
2. **Masturbation** – sex or sexual activity with self.
3. **Adultery** – sex or sexual activity of a married person with someone other than their own husband or wife.
4. **Incest** – sex or sexual activity with a close relative.
5. **Homosexuality** – sex or sexual activity with the same sex.
6. **Prostitution** – sex or sexual activity for money or personal gain.

7. **Pornography** & **Sexual Fantasy** – watching, listening to, reading or daydreaming about sex or sexual activity.
8. **Rape** & **Pedophilia** (child molestation) – forced sex or sexual activity and/or sex or sexual activity with someone who is underage.
9. **Bestiality** – sex or sexual activity with an animal.
10. **Sexual Lust** & **Lasciviousness** – craving for and strongly desiring sex or sexual activity, even though you know it's wrong; complete lack of self-restraint.

I would love to give you a detailed breakdown of these 10 spirits. The information is so deep and enlightening. However, it is too intense to write about in this book. That is why I write about these spirits in the other book I told you about. You will have to get that one in order to really get a full understanding of how these spirits operate – and you really do need this information!

I do at least want to tell you this though, sexual demons don't just influence your sexual behavior – they affect your ENTIRE life. Did you know that sex demons affect your personality, your friendships, and even your relationship with God?

For instance, people who are really strung out on masturbation are very selfish. The spirit of masturbation not only causes that person to sexually gratify their own bodies, but it gives the person a selfish mindset. A person who masturbates thinks that they are always right about everything; they are very critical and judgmental; they tend to like to be alone or do things on their own without anyone else's help. This is also the spirit that prevents people from being able to focus in prayer and worship for an extended time.

Let's talk about the spirit of fornication. The spirit of fornication causes you to engage in illicit and improper sexual activity.

However, it also causes insecurity, arrogance, and disloyalty. This spirit prevents people from being in a secure relationship with God – people who often backslide.

Let me give you one more – the spirit of prostitution causes you to have sex for personal gain. People think that you are only a prostitute if you stand out on a street corner and solicit sex for money. But that's not the only way that the spirit of prostitution can work in someone's life.

If you want to date the captain of the football team or of the cheerleading squad because of the status you will gain – that is prostitution. If you stay in a sexual relationship with someone just because they are paying your bills – that's prostitution too.

The spirit of prostitution prevents people from receiving love. No matter how much you try to love them, they cannot receive it. It breeds low self-esteem and destroys self-worth. The influence of this spirit also prevents people from receiving God's love.

- Adulterers are sneaky liars.
- People involved in incest are secretive and weird.
- Homosexuals struggle with who they are and are argumentative.
- People who watch pornography or have a lot of sexual fantasies are disorganized and procrastinate.
- Rapist and child molesters are control freaks and often violent.
- People involved in bestiality are hateful and usually involved in occultism.
- Those bound by sexual lust are greedy and untrustworthy...

Oh how I wish I could go on, but you will have to get **"The Spirits of Sexual Perversion Reference Book"** to learn the rest! If you have ever asked yourself, "What's wrong with me?" you need to read that book. You'll never see people or sex the same again after you read it.

Anyhoo – let me tell you before I go any further that all ten of those things that I named are sin! There is a lot to be said in today's society about what is "okay" in terms of sex. Right now the only thing that is off limits in this country is rape and molestation. Other than that – you are free to do whatever sick thing comes to mind.

But don't be fooled my friend. When you don't do it Yah's way – the consequences are steep. Don't believe all of the media hype and that fake stuff you see in music videos.

Sex is dangerous; sex hurts; and sex can kill – not just your body, but even worse, your soul...

~ Chapter 7 ~

The Game Plan

his chapter is named, "The Game Plan" because I really want to give you the inside scoop on the devil. He uses many different tricks and devices as weapons against us, but he does have his favorites. Looking at my own life and through observing the downfall of other people, I would have to say that his two favorite methods of spreading STDs are: **Promiscuity** and **Soul Ties**.

The 10 spirits of sexual perversion that I just listed off in the last chapter are the most likely STDs that will be transferred during sex. The devil is most interested in making sure you pick up these demons. The reason is that these are the ones that most effectively destroy your ability to have a close relationship with Yahweh God. However, there are many other demons that you can pick up through sex.

Just like with natural stds[5] (<u>s</u>exually <u>t</u>ransmitted <u>d</u>iseases), spiritual STDs are most easily spread through promiscuity. As a matter of fact, I don't think that it is a coincidence that the initials "STD" can stand for "sexually transmitted diseases", or "sexually transmitted demons". There are actually quite a few parallels between how natural stds and spiritual STDs work in your life.

---

[5] I will use lowercase letters, in the rest of the book, when referring to natural 'stds' for the sake of clarity.

Promiscuity means: *"Lacking selectivity or discrimination, especially when referring to a number of different sexual partners".*

One thing you will definitely learn in sex education class is that your risk of contracting an std increases, with an increase in sexual partners. The same is true in the spirit. Promiscuity was a huge factor in my life. I was not choosy about who I had sex with. My unspoken motto was, *"Whoever, whenever, where ever – let's just have sex!"* My lack of selectivity exposed me to so many STDs. That is why my life was so messed up by the time I got Born Again.

Earlier in chapter two, I told you that I was going to explain more to you about how two people become one through sex. Let me do this now, so you can understand how promiscuity is such an effective way to spread STDs. *(Remember, we are still talking about "Sexually Transmitted Demons" when I use the upper case letters.)*

The Bible teaches us that having sex actually causes you and your sex partner to become **ONE** *(1 Cor 6:16)*. You are literally **joining** yourself together with whomever you have sex with. During a wedding ceremony, the preacher says, *"We are gathered here today; to join together this man and this woman..."* Having sex is really a marriage without the wedding ceremony. That is why I wrote, you enter into a covenant (or contract) with whomever you have sex with.

We talked about **BLOOD** covenants earlier, and how they are the strongest covenants that can be made. Did you know that an erect penis is only hard because it is full of **BLOOD**? Did you know that the **BLOOD** vessels in a woman's vagina swell and increase in volume when she is aroused? A girl's cherry can only be popped once, but there is a **BLOOD** covenant that is created every time a sexual act takes place. Without the flow of **BLOOD** there could be no sex.

Sex is all about – <u>BLOOD</u> – <u>COVENANT</u> – <u>ONENESS</u>

The Bible says that *life is in the **BLOOD**. (Lev 17:11)* Because there is an exchange of blood during sex, through sexual activity you are literally joining your *life* together with the *life* of your sex partner. You are contracting with that person to make an exchange – just like how at a wedding ceremony the bride and groom "exchange vows".

I just want you to consider for a moment how the male and female bodies are made. They are created like interlocking puzzle pieces. When the pieces of a jigsaw puzzle are separated, all you see are a bunch of scattered pieces. But once you "lock" the pieces together, you have "ONE" picture. In the same way, when a man and woman are locked together in intercourse, they become "ONE". That is why it is so easy for sexual diseases to be spread through intercourse – whether vaginal, anal or oral. The insertion of the penis into the hole creates a oneness. It allows for easy access between the two bodies that have been joined together. Whatever is in one body can then be easily passed to the other body.

With spiritual STDs it's even worse though. To spread spiritual STDs, intercourse is not even necessary. The Bible says that we have already committed a sexual act in our hearts, even if we just look at someone with lust in our hearts. *(Mat 5:23)* That is why I wrote earlier that *any kind* of seXXXual activity can cause the spread of STDs – even stuff like hot kissing and phone seXXX.

I know this is deep, but – *stay with me, stay focused*!

I am saying that your body does not even have to make contact with the other person's body, in order for that contract to be made.

Lusting after someone to the point of arousal causes your spiritual body to be joined to theirs. Once you become aroused (which is just an excess of blood, or **life,** in the genital area), if you make no effort to suppress that arousal, the blood is released and a binding connection is made. The exchange of demons is then possible.

This is why promiscuity is such a powerful tool. The demon of promiscuity influences you to make that spiritual connection with person, after person, after person... In this way, satan can ensure maximum exposure to every demon of hell. He wants you to engage in seXXXual activity with as many people as is humanly possible, without being selective.

Promiscuity is also the spirit that influences provocative dress – you know – those tight jeans and low cut shirts. What do people say when someone is dressed provocatively? They say, *"You look* **SEXY.***"* Do you know why they say that? They say that because provocative dress causes sexual arousal – it causes that release of blood, the connection of two lives, which permits the exchange of STDs.

Provocative dress also draws attention to you. When dressed provocatively, you are more likely to be propositioned for dates. You know good and well that most of these dates will end in sex. And if you are a fella, don't think that only us chicks can dress provocatively! You can be provocative too – with your muscle shirts, tight jeans and biker shorts!

So now that you understand more about how sexual activity causes oneness and a spiritual connection, let's dig a little deeper into what happens when you make these sexual covenants with people. Remember that you learned earlier that a blood covenant can only be broken by death, or a new blood covenant. So what does that mean in terms of you having sex with multiple people?

If you stop having sex with a person and then move on to a new sexual partner, you create a new covenant and the oneness with the first partner is severed. If you completely disconnect from the first person, the exchange of demons with that person stops and you go through a separation, similar to how people separate before they get divorced. *(This is not the case if you continue to have sex with the person.)*

You need to realize though that just because you separate from someone that you have had sex with, it does not mean that they take their demons back. The demons you gained during the relationship are yours to keep. You aren't cured of Chlamydia just because you stop having sex with the person who gave it to you; and neither do you get free of a demon just because you stop having sex with the person you received it from.

What you may not realize is that you not only receive demons when you have sex, but you probably give some away too. Your partner will keep those demons when the relationship ends. However, as long as you remain in the relationship with the person, all of the demons are "community property". You and your sexual partner share them equally.

When you violate the covenant by having sex with a new person, you begin the separation and divorce process, but **Divorce Is Messy**. When two people get married, everything they have becomes "jointly" theirs. This means that they share everything. Nothing is exclusively "his" or "hers". Everything is "theirs". When they divorce, trying to divide everything that has been joined together is impossible. It is messy and destructive, especially when you start talking about children – *or in the case of STDs, demon spawn.*

It may sound good that you "give demons away", the less the better, *right?* However, even though demons are bad, they can become an significant part of your life. What I mean by this is that after you have a certain deficiency for so long, you get used to it. It becomes a part of who you are; part of your identity. Letting go of a deficiency can be hard because change is hard. When a marriage ends, community property cannot be shared anymore. Only one person can get the house, the dog, the car, etc... It is the same way spiritually. Those shared familiar demons must be separated.

The loss of those familiar demons that have become such an integral part of your life, leaves you feeling empty inside. If you think about it, even when a really bad relationship ends, the people that were involved still experience loss, depression and emptiness. Sometimes, it is not the person that you are missing; it is the spiritual energy of those demons that left with the person.

The man and woman involved in a divorce each walk away having gained some things and lost some things. Neither of them will ever be able to go back to being what they were before they got married. When they are torn apart by divorce, the blood that had become one must stop flowing. The life force that was being shared and exchanged between them is cut off. The separation is bloody – like trying to separate Siamese (conjoined) twins.

This is what happens spiritually when you switch sex partners! When conjoined twins are separated, both of them can be in danger of death. Each twin – because they are fused together – will lose skin, tissue, muscle and bone when they are separated. *If* the separation is successful, neither of them will ever be completely whole.

With promiscuity causing you to experience this terrible and painful phenomenon *over and over and over again*; it leaves you feeling totally confused and utterly empty. I like to describe promiscuity with the following example. You and every person you have sex with are each like a 5,000 piece jigsaw puzzle. Now think of approximately how many people you have had sexual contact with. Now think of mixing all of those different puzzles together and trying to sort them out!

Then you have to keep in mind that if the people you have had sex with, have had sex with others; they were already jumbled when you met them. The people they had sex with may have been jumbled already too. *Oh my Lord, what chaos and confusion this causes!* Your entire world consists of the fragmented pieces of the many wounded, wicked and dysfunctional spirits you have sexed. You do not even have all of your own pieces anymore, and yet you contain a multitude of fragmented mess that should not be there. This is a picture of complex confusion.

There are also some situations where two people don't get divorced, but someone in the marriage is being unfaithful. Or thinking again about the example of the Siamese twins – sometimes the twins are so fused together that they cannot be separated. What I mean is, just because you enter into a new blood covenant through sex, it does not necessarily mean that the former covenant is broken. As a matter of fact, more than likely, it is not broken at all. You can be in multiple contracts at one time – just like a husband or a wife can be cheating with many different sex partners, and yet still be married. Or even worse, how a person can be illegally married to more than one person at a time.

Sometimes married people get "separated", even though they are still legally married. They are no longer *joined*, but they are still in contract. Separation of a married couple can happen when the couple chooses to live a part, or even just through them refusing to engage in sexual activity for a long time. In other words, separation can "just happen". But divorce is a deliberate action that a person has to make a decision to pursue and follow through on. That is the only way to be completely free of the obligations of the marriage contract that was made.

This is the case spiritually too. You may feel like you are really *over* someone that you are no longer in relationship with, but spiritual divorce doesn't "just happen". You will be spiritually connected to a person, indefinitely, until full spiritual divorce takes place. *(You will learn how to do this in chapter 9)*. The person, and all of their demons, will still have full legal rights to you and all things concerning you. Remember, in marriage everything is *jointly owned*.

If a man separates from his wife but never goes through the courts to obtain a legal divorce, he will remain legally bound to her. If 30 years of separation passes and even if he illegally marries another woman – at his death it is his *legal* wife that will have the rights to his estate. This is very important to understand because as long as you are still in that spiritual marriage, the person still owns you, and you them.

At any given time, without warning or permission, that person's spirit can exercise his or her legal right to joint ownership of your life. Which means that if the person is still serving sin and satan, the devil has access to your life at all times through that covenant. Not only to you, but to whomever it is that you are currently having sex with as well, and anyone that you have had or ever will have sex with. Every person that you become one with and enter into covenant with will be tied to every other person that you are still in covenant with. **WOW...**

Are you feeling disoriented and confused? Do you feel empty inside and yet overwhelmed at the same time? That's the spirit of promiscuity at work in your life. All of the exchanges of demons and souls, the many messy divorces and the marriages that never ended...

WOW, I am always blown away when I read this chapter. Let's talk about it some more...

So you've learned that spiritual STDs can be spread without physical contact, through lusting after a person and provocative dress. Even though this is true, actual vaginal intercourse will always allow for the most powerful transference. Because of the closeness involved with vaginal intercourse, the emotional bonding that often happens, and the repeated activity – it allows for deeper connections to be made, and greater risk for the transfer of demons.

I can once again compare this to stds. You may have sex with someone that has AIDS and not get the disease. However, the more you have sex with that person, the more likely it is that you will eventually get HIV. I know of a couple in which the husband had AIDS. They managed to have sex for 10 years before the wife got infected. *You may get by for a while, but you keep playing with fire, you will eventually get burned.*

But there is something else that happens when you have sex many times with the same person. The more sexual intercourse you have with a person, the more you connect not only in spirit, but also in soul. When your soul bonds with someone else's soul, a fusing together of souls happens. When this happens, it is called a soul tie. Sex is not necessary for a soul tie to occur, but it is practically a given that a soul tie will be developed when you have sex with a person.

Your soul is considered your mind, your will and your emotions – your intellect, your desires and your feelings. You can be soul-tied to a person, place or thing and even to a demon. In other words, you can be mentally, emotionally and/or willfully bonded. A soul tie occurs when you have some type of void in your life. You try to fill this void by tying your soul to someone or something. Having sex leaves all types of voids in your life.

After you become sexually active, you are likely to form all kinds of unhealthy soul ties – trying to fill the voids that are created through the constant making and breaking of marriage covenants. This is another reason that it can be painful to lose the presence of familiar spirits (demons) that have been in your life. Demons are very skillful at affecting you on an emotional level and know very well how to create a bond with you.

Because you are not aware of the presence of these demons, you may not realize that this is what is happening. However, you can see the results of it when the relationship break up occurs. The scripture says that when a spirit leaves *(a void)*, he comes back with seven spirits more wicked than himself, and you will be worse off than you were before the spirit left. *(Luke 11:26)* So often times, after a break up, people's lives become even worse and they get involved in a lot unhealthy lifestyle choices.

Another tremendous opening for soul ties to occur is the breaking of the bond between parent and child that happens when you start having sex. Not having Momma – and Daddy, *if you ever had one* – in your life the way they used to be, will create a tremendous void. You will try to fill this void with all kinds of things. That is why a person is supposed to stay with their parents and under their covering **until they get married** *(unless needing to relocate for school or career, or choosing a life of celibacy)*. Not just women, but men as well – need to stay at home. In this way, the void that is created by the breaking of the bond with your parents will be immediately filled by your husband or your wife.

If done properly, a person's first sexual experience will create a soul-tie to the husband or wife that they will be married to for life. This is healthy and good and beautiful – and unfortunately, *uncommon*. When done this way, it leaves no room for satan to fill your soul up with detrimental ties that instead of anchoring you, imprison you. That is why the devil tries to make young people so anxious about getting out on their own. He knows that separation from your parents will cause you to form unhealthy soul ties.

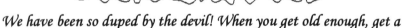

We have been so duped by the devil! When you get old enough, get a job and start contributing to your parents' household expenses. Gradually increase what you give to their household until you are paying enough to support your own household. Tithe 10%, sow your seeds, live off of 10%, pay bills in your parents' home and put the rest in savings. This is how you prepare for adult, married life – not by leaving, "sowing your wild oats" and living wastefully. If you do it this way, it will be a joy to your Mom and/or Dad for you to stay at home with them. Furthermore, you will preserve both your body and your soul for a wonderful, happy married life in the future!

If you are like most of us, that advice is probably coming too late, so let's talk more about soul ties. A soul tie can only be broken by discovering that it exists, and then filling the void with a replacement. I know in my own life, I had soul ties to people that I had not seen in years. Even people that I never really liked, I was still soul-tied to them. Those people had filled voids in my life, and once they filled their spot, to release them would have left me empty. I longed for seasons of my life that had passed, so I held on, not even realizing what I was doing. Most of the time, we are not aware of our soul ties.

Do you still think about someone that you had sex with a long time ago? Do you longingly reminisce on scenes or things from the past? That is a soul tie.

Soul ties can happen **as a result** of having sex with someone, or they can **be the reason** that you have sex with someone. A soul tie can trick you into thinking that you are "in love" with a person – making you want to tie together physically, in the same way that you are tied together in soul. Soul ties often lead people into sexual (and even homosexual) relations between friends. They often cause two people to get married for the wrong reasons. These marriages are miserable and empty and usually end in divorce. But my main point is that soul ties allow for the transference of demons. That is why I am mentioning them.

Basically, anytime you are connected to a person: physically, mentally, emotionally, or spiritually – you are soul-tied to that person. That connection allows for the transfer of demons.

You may tend to think that people will only be soul-tied to something that makes them happy, but that is not the case. You can have a negative soul tie to things as well. Even unforgiveness and bitterness is a type of soul tie. When you are bitter, you are tying your soul to some unpleasant event from your past and holding onto it. Unforgiveness can also lead to transference, which is why people often take on the nature of someone they hate – *they are soul-tied.*

People usually break up for unpleasant reasons, creating the opportunity for negative soul ties. Most people are NOT happy about a break up! Essentially what this means is that the same type of painful separation that occurs in your spirit will occur in your soul as well, when a covenant is broken or violated. Along with the tearing of the spirit that happens when a relationship ends, your soul will be stretched and twisted and yanked and pulled – you will feel scattered and that is simply because... **YOU ARE!**

Hmmm... It's something to think about, isn't it?

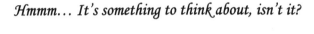

~ Chapter 8 ~

It's Just Not Worth It

June of 1997; I had an epiphany – **IT'S JUST NOT WORTH IT**. That day I'd had enough of my drunken boyfriend's nonsense! *Can I just say this like I felt it? "He was really a jerk!"* God rest his soul because he's dead now, but he was living in my house and yet not contributing anything to the bills. He made like $700 a week, but on payday he would never make it home until – LATE. He would drink up almost his entire paycheck.

By the time he got in; he was broke; reeked of liquor; would grope and lick on me like some dirty old pervert; spend the night making love to the toilet; and then wake up in the morning cursing me out because he had a hangover. Our life together was really miserable and pathetic. He was good for me in one sense though. My fear of a beat down kept me faithful. In other words, at least I was only sexing one dude for a change. I told you, my fear of pain was the one thing that could empower me to say no.

Not having sex with so many people started to clear up at least some of the confusion that was brought on by promiscuity. During a brief moment of clarity, I remembered how much I loved school. I always wanted to be a business woman, so I decided to go to college. Being around intelligent and intellectual people at school – I dreaded going home to him. He was an exceedingly ignorant person. Almost everything that came out of his mouth was utter nonsense. Our relationship was one of those "soul tie" things I told you about.

We met at a time when we were both experiencing tragedy. We were both homeless. His music studio that he lived in had burned down, leaving him homeless. I was homeless by choice because I decided that prostitution and motherhood didn't work too well together. I wanted to live a better life for the sake of my son, who was about one at the time.

Dude had actually been trying to get with me for a minute; I mean for about a year at least. I was not trying to hear it though. During the time that I met him, I was really into hip-hop. I used to be rapping in every studio in Queens, and that is how we met. One night I was in his studio really late. I didn't feel like taking that long train ride back to the Bronx at 1:00 in the morning, so I slept there.

He was drunk, as usual. He passed out in his underwear, and *his manhood* popped out when he rolled over. After I saw him in that condition, I didn't want anything to do with him. Growing up with a grandfather that was a drunk and many alcoholic relatives, I had no desire to be associated with addiction. I did not intend to ever give this guy a chance, but when we both ended up homeless, a soul tie was formed.

I was so lonely and afraid; living in a homeless shelter in Bronx, NY with my baby boy. One day Dude came all the way to the Bronx on the train to see me. This was about a 90-minute hike, plus a ten-block walk, to boot! I had no food, so he brought me $10 and walked me to the store. I bought some bread, farina, sugar, bananas and Kool-Aid *(LOL, I can still remember exactly what I purchased.)* Then we smoked a blunt he had brought with him. He walked me back to the shelter and took his long ride back to Queens.

I was hooked on him – or should I say "soul-tied" – after that. I thought that he cared, and that was the one thing missing in my life. There was always a lot of physical contact, but no real closeness – sex, but no intimacy. As turned off as I was by his constant drunkenness, ignorance and homelessness, I still became his girlfriend. I'm telling you, so many bad relationships are created because of soul ties. That is why we all need to be whole, no voids, nothing missing, nothing broken.

Anyway... One and a half years after we started dating, I was really fed up with his drinking and his ignorance. The soul tie was not strong enough to make me want to stay in the relationship. So on that day in June of 1997, I waited for him to get home from work so I could tell him that I wanted him to leave. We had argued on the phone before he came home. He knew what was coming. He came home nice and drunk to prepare for it. It was an ugly scene.

He had physically abused me before, but nothing like what was about to happen. He gave me one of those good, old-fashioned beat downs. He gave me one of those, *"If I can't have you, won't nobody have you!"* beat downs. I had never broken up with him before. I was the only thing that he had in life. I guess the thought of losing me was more than he could handle.

His "love" was more than I could handle. He beat me like I was a man. He punched and kicked and body slammed me. It was pretty pathetic because I am only five feet and weigh about 110 pounds. He was about six feet, two inches and weighed about 220 pounds. He had big fists too – EVERYTHING on him was big. After he beat me like that for a while, I was near unconsciousness. He had already punched my face into the stairs and broken my nose. I was out for the count, so I thought he was going to leave me alone, but then...

...It's so hard to write about this – deep breath – OK here it goes...

Then he picked me up. He threw me up against a wall and used one hand to hold me there. The other hand he drew back and used to make a fist. He was preparing to punch me square in the face with my head pressed against a concrete wall. And that's when I had it – the EPIPHANY, I mean. As my life flashed before my eyes that is when I realized that – IT'S JUST NOT WORTH IT! His fist was more than half the size of my entire face. That punch either would have killed me, or left me permanently deformed and brain-damaged.

I know that The LORD intervened because for no apparent reason at all, instead of punching me, he suddenly let go of me. My body slithered down the wall to the floor, as he turned and ran away. It's amazing how fast your mind works when your adrenaline is pumping like that. At that moment, I was so clear in my mind about how I had squandered my life.

In the following days as I healed, I really thought about my life. I cried, and I cried, and I cried. I am sure some of my sadness was due to the fact that this man that I had lived with for over a year would try to kill me. And some of my tears were shed for the physical pain that I was in. However, most of the tears I shed were for the life I had wasted. What kind of legacy would I have left if I had died that day? A legacy as *"a sexable freak that would easily give up the goods"*? That is all that I had accomplished in my life ever since I was 15 – I had gained *"a reputation"*.

During my reflecting, I remembered how when I was eight years old, I was diagnosed with Lupus. The doctors told my Mom that I would not live to be 21. I spent more time in the hospital than at home. I was in constant, excruciating pain. Some days the pain was so bad that I just wished I would go into a coma. My body was crippling up because of the pain. I can remember at one point, the doctors wanted to put me in a wheel chair because I walked so slowly, due to the pain. I fiercely protested.

I was in the fourth grade at that time. My classroom was on the second floor. I had to walk up and down the stairs every day for lunch and other activities. Since I refused the wheelchair, my teacher decided to help me out by having the janitor carry me up and down the stairs. I let him do it one time, but I was so humiliated that I never wanted him to do it again. I was determined to walk on my own!

The next day, I asked the teacher could I leave the classroom early so I could have extra time to walk to the lunchroom. She let me leave 15 minutes early. 15 minutes later, when the rest of the class was on their way to the lunchroom, I was still painstakingly making my way down the stairs. The teacher was so surprised when she saw me. I had tears in my eyes, but I mustered up a smile when I saw her. *"Laneen, are you alright? You sure you don't want me to call Mr. Johnson to carry you?"*

I wanted to scream at her; I wanted to curse her out, *"Can't you see that I am determined to do this on my own! Just go away and leave me with my dignity!!!"* That is what I was thinking, but I just gave her a teary-eyed smile and said, *"No Mrs. Brunson. I'll be down soon."* I cried every step of the way, but I made it on my own. By the time I finally made it into the cafeteria, lunch was almost over with. Nonetheless, I was determined to do it again the next day, and the next, and the next...

This was the type of determination and drive and fight that I had in me. I was supposed to be dead, but I was determined to live; I was supposed to be permanently brain-damaged after a fever of 109°, but I was determined to excel in school; I was supposed to be in a wheelchair, but I was determined to walk; I was never supposed to be able to have children, but I was determined to be a mother!

And in those days that followed that beating, as I thought about my life; my question to myself was, *"Do you mean to tell me that you made it through all of that just to end up like this? You survived sickness so you could die of whoredom? You dumb B#tch!"* It made me feel that I deserved that beating; a necessary "spanking" to shock me into a state of awareness. When I looked back over my life, I knew that the decline had started with sex.

I shook my head and said, "It's just not worth it." I was so angry with myself. All of the dreams that I had squandered; the wasted talents; the marred beauty...

I *could have* earned a scholarship to any college in the country; I *could have* written award-winning books; I *could have* been a model or an actress; I *could have* started a successful business...

With the determination, drive and God-given talents that I had – I "*could have*" done so much with my life. But instead, I had chosen to waste it on wild living – I chose to have sex before it was time.

Don't you know that God has something wonderful planned for your life? Thankfully, it was this tragedy that led me to salvation.

Now is your chance to learn from my mistakes. I won't lie to you and say that sex is not fun sometimes. Maybe you love sex. Maybe your story is not exactly like mine because maybe you do have wonderful orgasms and maybe you have never been molested or raped. Maybe you still have a decent relationship with your parents, are doing well in life, and enjoying school or a good job. Probably not for most people reading this book, but maybe *you* are the exception.

Or maybe... the devil has deceived you into thinking that you will be the one that actually gets away with it. Maybe he has tricked you into believing that you will be the one to never catch a spiritual STD or get spiritual AIDS. Perhaps you have been in a relationship with the same person for a while, having sex with only that one person, and you think that you are "okay".

If so, you may be saying, *"What does your story have to do with me?"*

Listen, our stories may not be the same, but the truth does not change. The truth is that STDs are real, and no one has illegal sex without getting AIDS! Most of the time you can't see STDs. It's just like not being able to see carbon monoxide gas when it leaks in a room. When carbon monoxide comes into the room, you can't see it, taste it, touch it, smell it, or hear it. But it is there, and it will quickly kill you. STDs are there, and they will – QUICKLY – destroy your life.

SEX CHANGES YOUR LIFE! That is the bottom line. Not only will you have to fight with demons that are directly transferred to you through sex, but there are other things that happen too. You will also have to deal with the hordes that come against you because of your separation from your parents; the life force that you lose during the "divorce" process; the many soul ties and twisted connections; and the constant open door for demonic oppression.

Worse of all – there is the curse of sin that no man can escape.

"...God is not mocked; for whatever a man sows, that will he also reap. (Gal 6:7)" "The wages of sin is death. (Rom 6:23)"

Another thing that people seldom consider is the long-term effects of their sexcapades. You know once you contract HIV; it doesn't go away just because you stop having sex. As I mentioned earlier, STDs are the same way. The hordes of hell that you invite into your life will stay with you. Long after you stop having sex; long after you realize that you have made a mistake; long after you decide that you want to change – your STDs will still be with you.

Just like natural stds – some spiritual STDs are easily cured, while others are incurable and stay with you for life. *And, you know what?* When I did research on sexually transmitted diseases, I found that a common symptom of severe std infection in the body is sterility. Sterility – meaning that you will never be able to have a baby. I am reminded again of the many parallels between natural stds and spiritual STDs. Sexually transmitted demons can make you sterile too – they can prevent you from being able to get pregnant with and give birth to your destiny!

Remember, I've told you from the very beginning that I am someone that you need to listen to. It may not seem like it, but **you can live without sex**. It's *with* sex that you may not be able to survive. Please trust me when I tell you...

...IT'S JUST NOT WORTH IT!

~ **Chapter 9** ~

Back Dat Thang Up!

When I thought that I had really ruined my life for good – just when I thought my suffering would never end – God stepped in again. Within a year of my fall with Elder Tony, Yahweh had completely turned my life around. My relationship with God and the calling on my life grew very strong, very quickly.

Around that time I met Emmanuel, the man who would become my husband. I was really sold out to God. I had finally allowed Yeshua to step in and be not only my Savior and Friend, but also MY LORD. I let Him have control of my life more each day, as I learned how to yield. I wish I could say that I never fell again after my encounter with Tony, but I did. I ended up getting engaged to his brother "Keith" *(at Tony's suggestion)*.

While Keith and I were engaged, we had sex. But I did notice a difference when I had sex with Keith. After having sex with him, I _knew_ that it was because of the spirits of sexual perversion that were in my life. I was sad that I messed up, but I was also confident that I would one day be delivered and walk in total victory. For the first time, I didn't let a slip into sexual sin send me running back to the world. I got up after falling, brushed myself off and kept pressing into Yahweh; pressing into my destiny; pressing into my purpose.

My hunger for righteousness and obedience made me more sensitive to The LORD's voice, and I was able to hear him when He told me to break off my engagement with Keith. That was a hard thing to do, especially giving back that $7,000 ring, but I wanted to be in the Father's perfect will more than I wanted anything. Yahweh saw my heart and that I was ready for change. After falling with Tony and Keith, I was so leery of falling again. I wanted to live a clean life so bad, but I still didn't know how to do that.

It is a truth that what we **want**, and what we are actually **prepared** for, are not always the same. I **wanted** to live in sexual purity, but I was not **prepared** to do so. I met Emmanuel shortly after breaking off the engagement with Keith. It had only been about a month since I had been sexually active. Emmanuel, on the other hand, had not had intercourse with a woman in nearly six years. I would never have pursued a man like him – I wouldn't even have thought that I had a chance.

But, I didn't need to pursue him because he pursued me. Once I realized that this man was really serious about marrying me; I knew that I had to tell him about my past. I spent about two hours one day – **truly bearing all**. I mean, I told him every hideous detail of my sexual past that I could think of. After I finished, I just hung my head down in shame and waited for the attack. But the attack never came. He looked me softly in the eyes and said to me, *"I am so sorry for what they did to you."* I had never felt more **accepted** in my entire life.

I was not attracted to my husband when I met him, nor was I interested in dating at all. All I could think about was trying to stay as far away from men as possible, to keep myself safe from sexual sin. However, just like the situation with the alcoholic that "I was not interested in", a soul tie was created with the man that would become my husband. He offered me acceptance, which I had never experienced from a man. Lack of acceptance was a terrible void in my life and he filled it, and that was all it took to get me to the altar.

One of the things that the enemy used to trick me into my marriage was my ignorance about what seXXXual activity really is. With Keith, I prayed about our engagement because we had full intercourse, and I knew it was wrong. The sex with Keith caused me to question whether he was really right for me.

But with Emmanuel, he never penetrated me before our wedding night. Now notice that I didn't say we didn't *have sex*, I just said that he never *penetrated* me. We did everything that we could possibly do sexually without him penetrating me. Unfortunately, I did not realize at that time that those acts were actually seXXX and fornication. I was still a babe at the time, having only been out of a backslidden state for a couple of months.

Emmanuel seemed so pure to me, but he was addictied to porn and masturbation *(a testimony he shares openly)*. It seemed noble that he had abstained from intercourse, but it was not because he was pure. It was because he preferred to live out his addictions alone and in secrecy. The excessive foreplay that we engaged in was nothing compared to his fantasies; nothing compared to the life I had lived.

This is why I said that what I wanted – a life of sexual purity – I was not prepared for. My idea of seuxal purity was any life that was better than the one I had been living. I am sure you can imagine that by those standards, I could do a whole lot, and still think that I was sexually "pure". I didn't even know what seuxal purity was at that time, so how could I possibly walk in it?

Some people , especially certain church leaders, mock and judge me because of the openness and rawness of this book. But my image is the last thing that I am concerned about. **MY GOAL IS TO MAKE SURE YOU KNOW EVERYTHING THAT I NEVER DID**. Had I realized that what I was doing with Emmanuel was sinful, I doubt I ever would have become his wife. Had I been able to see the level of perversion operating in him, He never would have been my husband. I would have prayed about it and broke it off, just as I did with Keith.

I was far from ready to be anybody's wife at that time, nor was he ready to be anybody's husband. Standing at the altar on our wedding day, I knew that he was not in love with me. I didn't feel any fondness toward me coming from him at all. There was no closeness, no oneness. In each other, we saw an escape from a life of sexual sin. Little did we know that STDs follow you everywhere, *even to the altar and even to the marriage bed.*

We became aware of this truth not until 11 years later, when we signed our divorce papers. Yet I am grateful that I went through this trial with someone like him, instead of someone like Keith. And truthfully, there is nothing in me that believes that I would have maintained a life of sexual purity, if I had remained single. After Tony and Keith and Emmanuel there probably would have been others, for years to come. My marriage was used to preserve me and to give me a safe place to work out my sexual addictions and strongholds.

I was very far from delivered though. In my desire to live right, I made a hasty decision to marry a man that was not my ordained husband. But even in my anxiousness and lack of wisdom, The LORD protected me because He saw my heart and that I was ready to change. He didn't allow me to marry a slacker like Keith. I married a Christian Minister, who I would go on to have six beautiful children with. Although our marriage ended, I had the opportunity to experience many years of growing as a Proverbs 31 wife, and today I have a good friend and a man that I am blessed to have as the father of my children. *"...All things work together for the good of them who love the Lord and are the called according to His purpose.(Rom 8:28)"*

I'll never regret my time as a wife, but I should never have tried to *go forward*, without first backing up. That is why I am saying to you that it is time to "back dat thang up", *as they like to say in hip-hop songs, LOL.* Back up the train of your life. It may have gotten off track, but it is not too late to back it up. You can still get on the right track and become all that you were destined to be. You do not have to remain a slave to sex. The information that you are about to read is what you need to know, in order to move forward with a successful life.

Hopefully I have convinced you by now; hopefully you believe me now when I tell you that it's just not worth it. **SeXXX** is not worth it. Are you still a virgin? Stay one! Have you lost your virginity? Recycle it! Are you sexually inexperienced? Good – don't try to become a pro! Are you really sexually "out there"? That's okay; make a decision to break the cycle today! Have you been molested or raped? It wasn't your fault – don't let a tragedy define who you are!

I made many terrible mistakes. I really thought that I had ruined my life for good... But Yahweh redeemed all of my mistakes and added value to my experiences. Not only did He heal me, but also *"He took my misery and turned it into ministry. He took my mess and turned it into a message."* In this chapter, I want to deliver another part of that message to you. I want to give you the twelve steps of deliverance that will lead you back into wholeness and purpose.

This deliverance process is really deep and involved. I can only give you a summary here, but it will be enough to get you started. Before I get into the 12 steps, I need you to know that "deliverance is a process, not an event". Every time I minister on deliverance, I let people know this. Deliverance is a progressive work. It is going to take:

- ✓ **Targeted Time** – Target your time to be spent on working out the 12 steps of deliverance; be focused not frivolous!
- ✓ **Passionate Purpose** – Put effort and energy into this process; do it with zeal and passion for the purpose of your destiny!
- ✓ **Concentrated Commitment** – Concentrate on being committed to seeing this thing through until you are victoriously free in every way!
- ✓ **Deliberate Determination** – Be deliberate about your determination; be tenacious and focused!!!

I pray that you will have some major breakthroughs **immediately** that will produce noticeable changes right away. But I don't want you to think that a few significant changes mean that you are totally delivered. A lot of people make that mistake and that is why their "so-called" deliverance will only last a few weeks or maybe a few months. I have been one of those people time and time again!

Don't watch the calendar to see how good you are doing. Your focus should not be on how fast or slow changes occur in your life. Your focus should be on living a new life, for the rest of your life – whether it takes six months for complete deliverance to occur or six years. Deliverance is not a "once and for all deal". Once you accomplish deliverance in your life, you have to maintain it; you have to keep walking in victory every day.

A simple definition of deliverance is "to be set free". One of the major factors in deliverance is understanding that as a person you are made up of three parts: spirit, soul and body. In order for total and true deliverance to happen in your life, you have to "be set free" in your spirit; in your soul; and in your body.

Your spirit is the truest essence of who you are. It is the core of your existence and the heart of your soul. Your soul is your mind, your will and your emotions. Your soul defines who you are on the earth. It contains your intellect and defines your personality. Your body is the most insignificant part of you, in terms of defining who you are. Without a spirit and soul, your body would just lay motionless and do nothing. Your body does not have the power that you may think that it does.

Since you are made up of three parts, I have divided the 12 steps of deliverance based on your three parts: Deliverance for your soul; Deliverance for your spirit; Deliverance for your body. So, now that I have laid all of the ground work – let's go over these 12 steps!

Deliverance for Your Soul

Step 1 – Confession Acknowledgement: The very first thing that you need to do is to acknowledge within yourself that you have a problem. This step is pretty straightforward and simple. This step is about keeping it real with yourself. You need to take a look at your life and check the way you are living. Even though this step is *simple*, it may not be *easy*. It is hard to see who we really are sometimes.

Step 2 – Discovery: This step is really, really important! This is about taking the time to figure out how you got so messed up. For example, why did I hate being a virgin so much at age 15? Why would I do something nasty like insert objects into my body? Those were demonic influences working in my life. No one just wants to do those things.

We don't grow up saying, *"I want to be a whore when I turn 15."* Or, *"I want to go to jail when I grow up."* Something happens to us along the way that puts us in bondage to satan and he begins to rule over our souls – twisting our intellect, contorting our emotions and conforming our will to match his.

Here are some of the things that happened in my life that caused me to be so messed up by the time I was a teenager: I was molested and raped at the age of two; I slept in the bed with older cousins who taught me how to masturbate; I had an uncle who let me watch pornography with him; I was abandoned by my mother when I was five (she came back for me, but I was already traumatized); my family smoked weed around me; I grew up without my real father; my stepfather was an adulterer and a child-molester; I almost died as a child; I was rejected by my peers; *yadda, yadda, yadda...*

The list is very long. *Guess what?* Everybody has a long list! Your list may be similar to mine. It might be really different, but **everyone has a list**. Discover what your list is because it is the things on that list that gives satan access to your life. In this discovery step, just know that there are four main ways that satan gets into your life to control and influence your behavior:

1. *Generational curses* – These are bad behaviors and negative

outcomes that run in the family. Pray for forgiveness for the sins of your family members, even the dead ones and then renounce these generational demons.

2. *Involuntary exposure* – This means being exposed to bad things when you can't help it. For example, being raised by a drug addict or being molested. Everyday just say out loud, *"Lord I cover myself in the Blood of Yeshua. I renounce every demon that has come or will try to come through involuntary exposure."*

3. *Spiritual wounds* – This is when people hurt you; like being abandoned, abused or bullied in school – the stuff on your list. To get healing you must first and foremost forgive the people that have hurt you. Next, you must allow yourself to grieve in the presence of God. Don't try to pretend it doesn't hurt. It is important to cry to The Father. When you do, He will heal you.

4. *Voluntary exposure* – This is when you make a **deliberate decision** to do bad things or put yourself in bad situations. This type of behavior gives satan the greatest opening to your life because with voluntary exposure, **you invite him in**. This is also a form of witchcraft because you are deliberately rebelling against Yah. Ask for forgiveness and make a commitment to change in order to close the doors that you have opened through sin. Sin means *breaking Yah's law.*

Step 3 – Renewing the Mind: The Bible tells us that we will be transformed if we renew our minds. *(Rom 12:2)* Everything that you do begins with a thought. That is why if you are planning on changing your behavior, you are going to have to start with changing the way that you think about things. You have to put the right things into your mind, and keep the wrong things out.

Everything that you see, hear, touch, taste, and smell has an impact on how you think. This means that if you are going to renew your mind in a way that will allow you to be transformed into the type of person that you want to become, you will have to stop putting in the same old junk.

You can't watch nasty movies, and listen to nasty songs, and read nasty books, hang around nasty people, and wear nasty clothes; and expect to have clean thoughts! Come on – don't kid yourself! Watch Christian programs, read your Bible, listen to Gospel music, go to church – and this is especially important – work on memorizing scriptures and quoting them when you feel weak.

Deliverance for Your Spirit

Step 4 – Confession Admittance: The first part of confession is between you and yourself. This second part of confession is between you and God. It is not enough to just "know" that you have a problem. Once you know, you need to confess your sins to Yahweh.

There is a scripture in the Bible that says if you confess your sins to Yahweh He will be just and faithful to forgive you and cleanse you of all wickedness. *(1 John 1:9)* You can't be forgiven if you don't first confess. And please, be real with Him when you make your confession. Don't beat around the bush and tell half-truths. He hates that. He already knows everything and is waiting to forgive and restore you; but you have to be honest.

Step 5 – Penitence/Humility: The Bible says that Yahweh will not despise a contrite heart and a broken spirit. *(Ps 51:17)* This means that when you confess to Him, it needs to be done with brokenness and humility. Have you ever apologized to someone just because you were told to, but you weren't really sorry in your heart? That is what we do to God sometimes! You will not experience deliverance if you do not have brokenness and remorse for your sins. You have to really be sorrowful and willing to change. **TRUE REPENTANCE IS FOLLOWED BY CHANGE.**

Step 6 – Confession/Exposure: The first part of confession was between you and yourself; the second part was between you and Yah; this third part is between you and people. You need to find another Christian who is really living a clean life, that won't gossip and knows how to pray. Let that person know about what is going on in your life. Telling someone else about your struggles is going to do two things: 1) It is going to make you accountable for your actions; and 2) It will allow that person to be able to pray for you, in order to help strengthen you.

One of the main reasons people stay in bondage is because they have a victim mentality. I love this quote, *"Life is 10% what happens to you, and 90% how you respond to it!"* This is so true, so true, so true... Confess your faults to someone; and share with them your plans for change. Take responsibility for your actions as they pray for you. Ditch the victim mentality and *choose to be an overcomer*.

Step 7 – Forgiveness and Letting Go: If you want to be free – you are going to have to free other people. You have imprisoned people with your bitterness and unforgiveness. As long as you hold onto the past, your arms will be too full to embrace your future. If you don't let go of your bitterness, you can't receive Yah's sweet healing.

Step 8 – Putting on Your Spiritual Armor:

- *The belt of truth* – to protect yourself from shame, and guilty feelings.
- *The body armor of Righteousness* – being covered in Yeshua's

Righteousness instead of your sins, through His Blood.

- *The shoes of peace* – living in the peace of knowing that you are a Born Again Believer; in a right place with Yahweh God; and that He, through His Love for you, controls the outcome of your life.

- *The shield of faith* – use it to protect yourself from the enemy's attacks of temptation and failure.

- The helmet of salvation – know that salvation is a process that has to be walked out every day. *"He who endures to the end, shall be saved. (Mat 10:22)"*

Step 9 – Using Your Spiritual Weapons:

- *The sword of the Word* – The LORD's Word, which you can read in the Bible, can be used to cut down every demonic influence and attack in your life. Read it, study it, memorize it and become a skillful swordsman.

- *The power of praise* – Yahweh lives in the praises of His people. When you praise God, **you bring Him right into your situation** to defend you against satan.

- *Christian fellowship* – there is strength in numbers. Get together with other strong believers so that they can help you stand.

- *Prayer and fasting* – this is the most effective and powerful way to drive demons out of your life.

- *Taking communion* – partaking of The LORD's supper through the practice of communion is the most powerful way to connect with Yeshua. It is the only way to get a **complete spiritual divorce** from all previous marriages and break the connection that you have with your sex partners and their demons. Yeshua's Blood of the Covenant breaks all other covenants and connects you to Him intimately!!!

Step 10 – Retreat and Replenish: It is important to step back from the warfare and just refresh your spirit in the pureness of worship in Yahweh's presence. Don't burn yourself out. Even though it is called "spiritual" warfare, it still requires "physical" energy. *I will teach you more about worship in the next chapter.*

Deliverance for Your Body

Step 11- Discipline: Most of us hate this word; I know that it was never one of my favorites *(smile)*. However, discipline is not so hard to achieve once you work on deliverance for your soul and your spirit. Discipline is not *something that you **do***; it is a mindset and a nature that you take on. Set small discipline goals for yourself in order to gain self-control, as you are submitted to the Holy Spirit.

Step 12 – Walking After the Spirit: This step is about how you live your life from day to day. It is about offering your body up as a living sacrifice to Yahweh God. It is about being a light in a dark world and not giving into the pressures of temptation. You have to be willing to be different; willing to stand out and do what Yeshua did when He was on the earth. Remember that people are always watching you, so you need to watch yourself.

With everything you do; every step you take; every word you speak; ask yourself, "Will this glorify God? Will this bless The God of Holiness?"

~ Chapter 10 ~

Go Long, Go Deep, Go Hard

*G*o long – go deep – go hard... I know that title has you curious. *Perhaps another tale of my sexcapades?* No, not this time. This is the most important chapter of this book. Every person that is called into ministry leadership has a specific assignment – I mean, "a specialty". My specialty is teaching people the deeper truths about sex, sexual perversion and worship. You may be wondering how worship ties in with sex and sexual perversion. Sex has more to do with worship than you can imagine – it has everything to do with worship.

THE DEVIL WANTS TO STEAL YOUR WORSHIP!

That's what sexual sin is all about – the devil trying to steal your worship. This is something that I really address in great detail in my other book, ***"The Spirits of Sexual Perversion Reference Book"***. I must say again that I really encourage you to get it and study it. In the mean time, let me teach you a little about sex and worship now.

Everything that exists in life and on this earth, exists for the purpose of helping us understand our relationship with The Creator God. Everything in creation is pointing back to Yahweh as The Creator of All Things and our existence **in Him**. The ultimate purpose and destiny of every human being is to return to the God that created them.

You learned earlier that your existence began "**in Him, in Yahweh**". Then your existence in Him was interrupted for a short season so that He could give you a body and introduce you to time. In Him there is no time or distance. Yahweh is eternity, and He is infinity; He is in all and He is all.

You have been injected into time to do a work on this earth, but in order to sucessfully do what God has destined you to do – you must first re-connect with Him. You have to re-establish the covenant (contract) that you had with Him in eternity before you were born. He sent His Son Yeshua (Jesus), to shed His Blood on your behalf so that your blood covenant with The Father could be re-established.

I hope that you are already a Born Again Believer. If you aren't, there are some instructions on how you can become Born Again beginning on page 94. I suggest that you go there right now and give your life to Yeshua. Do it before you read the rest of this chapter. You won't be able to do what I will tell you to do in this chapter, if you are not Born Again.

What I want to tell you to do in this chapter is to – *go long, go deep and go hard.* I want to tell you to worship Yahweh God with all of your heart. You see sex was given to us as an illustration of intimacy with The LORD. Pure sexual intimacy between a husband and wife is a picture of pure spiritual intimacy between you and Your Creator. That is why I choose a sensual title for this chapter.

There are four things that Yah wanted to teach us about worship with Him, through the human intimacy of a husband and wife.

1) He wants us to know that we are to worship only Him. In a good marriage the husband and wife only have sex with each

other. The greatest violation that can occur is for one of them to have sex outside of the marriage.

2) Yah wants us to understand that through worship we strenghthen and re-establish our covenant with Him. Remember what you learned about the exchange of blood that takes place during intercourse? Everytime a husband and wife have sex, it is like they are re-newing their covenant with one another. The same thing happens spiritually when we worship God.

3) Yah wants us to understand the intimacy of worship in spirit. There is a difference between "making love" and merely "having sex". Having sex is a pleasurable physical experience but is empty of heart and soul. When a husband and wife who are truly in love have sex, they do it with their entire beings. It is not just a physical act, but instead is the Ultimate Physical Expression of a deep abiding love that comes from the spirit. This is the intimacy that God wants with us.

4) Yah also wants us to know that when we are joined together with Him in worship, we have creative power – just like a husband and a wife can create a baby when they have sex. Have you ever heard the clause of The Lord's Prayer that says, *"Thy will be done; Thy Kingdom come on earth as it is Heaven..."?* This prayer is fulfilled in worship.

That's powerful isn't it? Most people don't even consider the deeper purposes of sex. They think that it is just for their pleasure. And that is what the devil wants you to think. The Bible says that the devil is *"the prince of the power of the air"*. *(Eph 2:2)* He controls the airwaves of the media, and his desire to steal your worship is why he has saturated the media with sexual perversion.

The devil could really care less if you have sex, or masturbate, or cheat on your husband or wife. The sins that you commit with your body can easily be forgiven. Through a simple act of confession, whatever wrong thing you have done with your body is thrown into the sea of forgetfulness. What the devil is really after is **your understanding of worship**.

You may not realize it, but satan knows that if your understanding of sex is messed up; if you don't understand pure intimacy can only take place between a husband and a wife – then you will never really understand worship with The LORD God Almighty.

Yahweh is acutally looking for true worshipers. He wants you to worship Him in spirit and in truth – in other words, in pure nakedness. When two people are really into each other, they enjoy getting naked for sex. When you don't really feel comfortable with the person you are with, you may want to leave some of your clothes on. You may want to have the lights off to hide your body.

But Yahweh wants you to get naked before Him, and He wants to be naked before you. He wants you to *leave the lights on*, so He can reveal His true self to you. A lot of people get Born Again. The devil doesn't want you to get Born Again, but if you do – his next goal will be to keep you from ever entering into true worship. Many become Born Again, but not many ever become intimate worshipers of The Living God. Without true worship, you will never give birth to the destiny that The LORD has for you.

Remember, worship is like sex. Without medical technology, can a woman get pregnant without having sex? No, she cannot. She may have a million eggs in her ovaries, but if she never lays with her husband so he can fertilize those eggs with his sperm, she will never be pregnant with his child. Modern technology has made it possible for women to get pregnant by other means, but that option doesn't exist spiritually!

You have seeds of God's destiny and His Kingdom on the inside of you. But if you don't lay with Him in worship – if you don't allow Him to fertilize what He has placed in you with His Seed – you will never concieve or give birth to anything that He has placed on the inside of you. That is why satan does not want you to worship! He wants the filth of perversion to consume your thoughts; he wants the stench of sexual sin to rest on your body; he wants the stains of masturbation to cover your hands; he wants the perversion of pornography to fill your eyes and contaminate your imagination. He wants your heart to be so overwhelmed with lust that you will be guilt laden and unable to get naked before Yahweh and worship Him!

When Adam and Eve sinned in the Garden of Eden, the first thing they did was cover themselves. Their sin produced guilt and guilt kept them from being able to get naked with Yah in worship. That is why The LORD told Adam he would die if he ate the fruit from that tree. It was not because Yah planned to kill Adam. It was because God knew that guilt would prevent worship, it would prevent the exchange of life-force, the Blood of God's Spirit, that was necessary for the constant re-newing of the covenant that He had with Adam. "Life is in the Blood." *No blood – no life – death comes...*

I could get lost in that revelation, but let me stop. I just want to make an impact on your thinking. From now on when you think about sex, I want you to remember that sexual sin and perversion will kill your worship life with Yahweh God. From now on when you think about sex, I want you to relate those thoughts to worship and learn how to be intimate with Yahweh God.

The next time you feel your body crave and long for sex, I want you to understand that The Creator gave you the ability to have those sexual longings, so you would understand how bad He wants your worship. He hungers for your initmacy; He burns with desire for you. He wants to get inside of you. He wants to feel your presence. He wants to smell the breath of your praises and embrace you. He wants to explode inside of you and release His seed into you. He wants to go long, and deep and hard with you.

He loves you so much that He has called you the apple of His eye. He wants to dress you up in His blessings. He wants to write His name across your heart. He wants you to have His baby; give birth to His Kingdom. Yahweh wants your worship.

Overcome the temptations of satan because he has only come to steal, kill and destroy the abundant life that Yeshua came to give you. That abundant life starts with worship and satan does not want you to understand that worship. He wants you to think that God is a one night stand or a late night "booty call". The God that Created You does not want to just "bang you in the back of the club". He wants you for a life time.

He wants a wife, not a fling. Yahweh does not want to rape you, or molest you, or spank you, or hurt you in any way. His intimacy with you is tender and pure. He wants to take His time with you. He wants you to get undressed in front of Him, then He wants to slowly love on you. He wants to excite you and prepare your spirit for His entrance. He's not in a rush. He wants it to last a long time. He wants to go long, go deep and go hard with you.

If you are already sexually active, it won't be easy to stop. However, now that you know what that craving in your body is really for – give those feelings to God. Everytime you feel that urge in your loins, give yourself to the Lover of Your Soul, in worship.

What does it mean to worship? It means that you give yourself to Him. You give Him total control over your mind, body and soul. You submit completely to Him and let Him have His way with you. And know this, that in a good marriage, a husband and wife don't ignore each other all day and then fall into bed at night and "screw". They are intimate with each other all day long. All day they touch, hug, talk, smile and function together as ONE.

There is a constant, unbroken connection that goes on. The commitment that is between them as husband and wife is on their minds all day. The love that they feel for each other burns in their hearts. By the time they finally have a chance to be alone, there is a yearning to express physically what they have felt in their hearts all day. They are so ready for that sweet intimacy and physical connection to take place when the time finally comes. This is how it ought to be be with our worship, ready and on fire.

We give ourselves to so many things like that. We have so many idols that we worship. What do you think about all day long? What consumes your thoughts? What does your heart burn for? If it is not Yahweh God, you are worshiping idols. Who or what have you given yourself to that has taken God's place?

Worship Yahweh and worship Him alone. Worship Him with all of your heart. He yearns for you. He wants to connect with you. He wants to keep the covenant strong. He wants to get you pregnant with destiny. Give yourself to Him. Give Him total control over your mind, body and soul. Submit completely to Him and let Him have His way with you. Go long – go deep – go hard...

Start a New Life Today!

You must be a Born Again Believer in Yeshua Ha-Mashiach in order to truly live a life of freedom. The ultimate purpose and destiny of every human being is to be re-connected to the God that created them. The pathway to Yahweh God is through his Son Jesus Christ, or as He was originally named – Yeshua. The Bible says that the only way to have a relationship with The Father, whose name is Yahweh, is through His son Yeshua. So how do you become Born Again? You must: **KNOW, BELIEVE, ACCEPT** and **SERVE.**

First you must **KNOW** who Yeshua is. Yeshua is the Holy and sinless Son of Yahweh God. The Bible teaches us that the Father and the Son are one, and so although Yeshua is the Son; He also is God.

Second, you must **BELIEVE** the truth of the Gospel. Yeshua was born by the virgin Mary. She concieved Him by the Holy Spirit and not a man. Yeshua lived on the earth and performed great miracles as the Anointed One of God. He then willingly gave His life up, by being sacrificed on the cross. He shed His Blood for your sins. He died and after three days He was risen from the dead. After being risen, He stayed on the earth for 40 days and then ascended back into heaven to sit on the throne at the right hand of the Father.

Third, you must **ACCEPT** Yeshua as your personal Savior. In order to accept Yeshua as your personal Savior, you must confess out loud with your mouth what you KNOW about Him and what you BELIEVE about him. You must also confess that you are a sinner and that you need to be saved. You must ask the Father for forgivness in Yeshua's Name and be willing to change. You must invite Yahweh into your heart to be your Savior

Fourth, you must **SERVE**. The proof is in the pudding! If you really are Born Again, then you will allow Yeshua to be not only your Savior, but also your LORD. That means that you commit to let Him have control over your life from now on. It does not mean that you will never make a mistake, but you must live each day to serve Him from now on.

So, are you ready to get Born Again? Great! Then just say your own prayer to Yahweh God as I told you to do in the **ACCEPT** step. He'll give you the words to pray. Congratulations on becoming a part of the greatest clique on earth – The Body of Christ. Find a good church to go to and get baptized. Read your Bible and pray every day. I pray for you right now for the baptism of the Holy Spirit with the evidence of speaking in tongues!

Please leave a message on my website to let me know that you have become born again! Go to www.drintimacy.com and leave a message on the "Guest Book" page, or send me an e-mail. Thanks!

The most unique book ever of its kind, **"The Spirits of Sexual Perversion Reference Book: 2013 Edition"** delves deeply into the subject matter of God-designed sexuality, sexual sin and how sex is relative to our worship of God. It includes a dedicated chapter on "sex demons", also referred to as incubus. There is a new chapter for married couples. Along with these additions, you will find 11 different spirits of sexual perversion discussed in deep and insightful detail, each in its own designated chapter. Also, enjoy powerful application revelations in a section entitled *"Insights from Dr. Intimacy"*. Thousands of church leaders and lay people have received help in getting understanding and true deliverance concerning issues of sexual perversion. Many more, including those outside of the church, have been touched and encouraged by Laneen's transparency in sharing her powerful testimony. This is it! God's Textbook on Sex Education; The Encyclopedia of Christian Sexuality! Find out more about it on my website or order directly from Amazon.com today! Enjoy a special promo price just for reading this book. Visit this link www.drintimacy.com/Ref_Book_Promo.html.

About the Author

Prophetess Laneen Haniah, a prolific author and lecturer better known as "Dr. Intimacy", gives an enlightening look into the naked truth about sex, intimacy and worship from a holistic perspective. Her passion for this ministry was birthed out of peer pressure, troubles at home and a past of childhood molestation that led to a tumultuous life for Laneen. She shares these experiences in her books. Her two bestsellers have over 10,000 copies in print, each recognized by Writer's Digest. She has been a sought after conference speaker throughout the U.S., a popular talk radio show guest and has been featured in a number of magazines. She is also the creator of the popular *"Insights from Dr. Intimacy"* weblog and YouTube channel. Her ministry assignment is not about the mechanics of physical sex. It is about the intimate, inner workings of the spirit of humankind and how it connects to Yahweh God and all that He has created.

Dr. Intimacy currently resides in Dallas, TX with her seven children. She is a wellness consultant, recording artist and small business owner.

I'd love to connect with you!
Please visit my website! Find all
of my social media links and
donation infomration on the site.
Thanks for your support.
www.drintimacy.com